MW00669256

The Gospel of Matthew

HOPE IN THE RESURRECTED CHRIST

CAROL DAVIS YOUNGER
PERRY LASSITER
LEIGH ANN POWERS
ALBERT REYES

BAPTISTWAYPRESS®

Dallas, Texas

BAPTISTWAY PRESS® Management Team
Executive Director, Baptist General Convention of Texas: Randel Everett
Director, Missions, Evangelism, and Ministry Team: Wayne Shuffield
Ministry Team Leader: Phil Miller
Publisher, BAPTISTWAY PRESS®: Ross West

Cover and Interior Design and Production: Desktop Miracles, Inc.
Printing: Data Reproductions Corporation

First edition: December 2008
ISBN–13: 978–1–934731–14–7

How to Make the Best Use of This Issue

Whether you're the teacher or a student—

1. Start early in the week before your class meets.

2. Overview the study. Review the table of contents and read the study introduction. Try to see how each lesson relates to the overall study.

3. Use your Bible to read and consider prayerfully the Scripture passages for the lesson. (You'll see that each writer has chosen a favorite translation for the lessons in this issue. You're free to use the Bible translation you prefer and compare it with the translation chosen for that unit, of course.)

4. After reading all the Scripture passages in your Bible, then read the writer's comments. The comments are intended to be an aid to your study of the Bible.

5. Read the small articles—"sidebars"—in each lesson. They are intended to provide additional, enrichment information and inspiration and to encourage thought and application.

6. Try to answer for yourself the questions included in each lesson. They're intended to encourage further thought and application, and they can also be used in the class session itself.

If you're the teacher—

A. Do all of the things just mentioned, of course. As you begin the study with your class, be sure to find a way to help your class know the date on which each lesson will be studied. You might do this in one or more of the following ways:

   • In the first session of the study, briefly overview the study by identifying with your class the date on which each lesson will be studied. Lead your class to write the date in the table of contents on pages 7–8 and on the first page of each lesson.

- Make and post a chart that indicates the date on which each lesson will be studied.
- If all of your class has e-mail, send them an e-mail with the dates the lessons will be studied.
- Provide a bookmark with the lesson dates. You may want to include information about your church and then use the bookmark as a visitation tool, too.
- Develop a sticker with the lesson dates, and place it on the table of contents or on the back cover.

B. Get a copy of the *Teaching Guide*, a companion piece to this *Study Guide*. The *Teaching Guide* contains additional Bible comments plus two teaching plans. The teaching plans in the *Teaching Guide* are intended to provide practical, easy-to-use teaching suggestions that will work in your class.

C. After you've studied the Bible passage, the lesson comments, and other material, use the teaching suggestions in the *Teaching Guide* to help you develop your plan for leading your class in studying each lesson.

D. You may want to get the additional adult Bible study comments—*Adult Online Bible Commentary*—by Dr. Jim Denison, pastor of Park Cities Baptist Church, Dallas, Texas, that are available at www.baptistwaypress.org and can be downloaded free. An additional teaching plan plus teaching resource items are also available at www.baptistwaypress.org.

E. You also may want to get the enrichment teaching help that is provided on the internet by the *Baptist Standard* at www.baptiststandard.com. (Other class participants may find this information helpful, too.) Call 214–630–4571 to begin your subscription to the printed edition of the *Baptist Standard*.

F. Enjoy leading your class in discovering the meaning of the Scripture passages and in applying these passages to their lives.

Writers of This Study Guide

Carol Davis Younger wrote the unit one introduction and lessons one through three. She lives in Atlanta, Georgia, and is an experienced curriculum writer. Carol graduated from Baylor University with a degree in English and received a Master of Divinity degree from Southern Baptist Theological Seminary, Louisville, Kentucky. The Youngers have two sons—Graham and Caleb.

Perry Lassiter wrote unit two, lessons four and five. He is a member of First Baptist Church, Ruston, Louisiana. A graduate of Baylor and of Southern Baptist Theological Seminary, he served as a pastor for more than forty-five years and continues to preach and to serve churches as an interim pastor.

Leigh Ann Powers, writer of unit three, lessons six through nine, is a member of First Baptist Church, Runge, Texas, where her husband serves as pastor. She is a graduate of Baylor University (B.S.Ed.) and of Southwestern Baptist Seminary (M.Div.). She teaches an adult Sunday School class and works with the children's ministry at her church. She and her husband, Heath, have two children.

Albert Reyes is president of Buckner Children and Family Services, Inc., Dallas, Texas. Dr. Reyes wrote unit four, lessons ten through twelve, and the bonus lesson. Previously he served as president of Baptist University of the Americas, San Antonio; pastor of Baptist churches in Dallas and El Paso; and on the faculty of Baptist University of the Americas, Howard Payne University, George W. Truett Theological Seminary, Dallas Baptist University, and the Mexican Baptist Theological Seminary in Mexico City. He served as president of the Baptist General Convention of Texas and is a graduate of Angelo State University (B.B.A.) and of Southwestern Baptist Theological Seminary (M.Div., D.Min.). He also holds an honorary Doctor of Divinity Degree from Dallas Baptist University.

The Gospel of Matthew: Hope in the Resurrected Christ

UNIT THREE

Hope in Jesus' Teachings

UNIT FOUR

Hope in Jesus' Glorification

Introducing the Gospel of Matthew: Hope in the Resurrected Christ

Beginning at the End

"Life can only be understood backwards, but it must be lived forwards." So wrote the nineteenth-century Danish theologian Soren Kierkegaard. He was referring to the idea that often we understand our lives best as we look back, not as we attempt to live them "forwards."

Consider how that idea can be applied to the Gospel of Matthew, and indeed to all of the Gospels. The early Christians, including the first readers of the Gospel of Matthew, viewed the story of Jesus through the lens of God's exaltation of Jesus in Jesus' resurrection. They in a sense heard and read the story of Jesus as they looked "backwards." That is, the beginning point for their understanding Jesus and his story was not Jesus' birth, where the Gospel of Matthew begins, but Jesus' resurrection. For them, Jesus' exalted status as the crucified and resurrected Lord commissioning his disciples brought clarification and meaning to all the other events of Jesus' life. Studying Jesus' life and ministry from the viewpoint of Jesus' resurrection will do the same for us.

Remember that Matthew already knew the ending in Matthew 28 when he wrote Matthew 1. Indeed, he wrote Matthew 1—27 with the full knowledge of Jesus' resurrection in Matthew 28. Surely that magnificent reality affected Matthew's record of all the rest of the Gospel he wrote.

Therefore, the point of reference for this series of Bible study lessons and indeed an important perspective for understanding Matthew's Gospel as a whole is that it is the story of hope and celebration focused in the life, ministry, teachings, crucifixion, and resurrection of Jesus. The lessons in this study feature Scriptures that focus on this theme.

Although Jesus faced opposition even to the point of a horrible and horrifying death on a cross, the keynote of the story of Jesus is hope and celebration. The early church knew this. Let us learn it anew as we study these selected passages in the Gospel of Matthew.[1]

Approaching This Study

These lessons are the third study of Matthew that has been done in this series of Bible studies since the beginning in March 2000. Both previous studies are somewhat different in approach from this one, and both are still available (see www.baptistwaypress.org).

Another factor in this study of Matthew is that the curriculum plan for this series calls for a study of one of the Gospels each year. This feature is provided in order to help us stay in touch as much as possible with the life and teachings of Jesus, who is "the criterion by which the Bible is to be interpreted."[2]

So, in addition to focusing on Scriptures that lend themselves most readily to the theme of this study—hope and celebration in light of Jesus' resurrection—the attempt has been made to study passages not dealt with extensively or recently in previous studies of the Gospels. In selecting Scripture passages, attention has also been given to studying passages that are unique to the Gospel of Matthew or are treated in most detail there.

Note: The first use of this study in the churches begins in December 2008. Since December 2008—February 2009 has only twelve Sundays, the study provides twelve lessons. However, to meet the needs of churches and classes who generally expect at least thirteen sessions in our studies, we have included a *bonus* lesson—"Jesus and Hurting People," on Matthew 25:31–46. If your church or class uses the bonus lesson, you may find it fits best after either lesson nine (because it is part of Jesus' teachings) or lesson ten (because the Scripture passages come after the passages in lesson ten in the Gospel of Matthew). Whenever you use the lesson, you are encouraged to use it at some point because of the importance of its subject matter.

UNIT ONE. HOPE IN JESUS' BIRTH

Additional Resources for Studying the Gospel of Matthew[3]

Craig L. Blomberg. *Matthew.* The New American Commentary. Nashville: Broadman Press, 1992.

Dietrich Bonhoeffer. *The Cost of Discipleship.* New York: Simon & Schuster, Touchstone Book, 1995 (originally published in German in 1937).

M. Eugene Boring. "Matthew." *The New Interpreter's Bible.* Volume VIII. Nashville: Abingdon Press, 1995.

David Garland. *Reading Matthew.* Macon, Georgia: Smyth and Helwys Publishing, Inc., 1999.

Douglas R. A. Hare. *Matthew.* Interpretation: A Bible Commentary for Teaching and Preaching. Louisville: John Knox Press, 1993.

A.T. Robertson. "The Gospel of Matthew." *Word Pictures in the New Testament.* Volume 1. Nashville, Tennessee: Broadman Press, 1930.

Frank Stagg. "Matthew." *The Broadman Bible Commentary.* Volume 8. Nashville: Broadman Press, 1969.

NOTES

1. Unless otherwise indicated, all Scripture quotations in this introductory article are from the New Revised Standard Bible.

2. *The Baptist Faith and Message* (1963), article 1.

3. Listing a book does not imply full agreement by the writers or BAPTISTWAY PRESS® with all of its comments.

Hope in Jesus' Birth

Do you think of the word "hope" as a verb or a noun? Do you hear "Hope in Jesus' Birth" as a call to action, a call to keep placing your hope and trust in what God did in Bethlehem? Or do the words remind you of something that resulted from the event of Jesus' nativity, a treasure God gave us to hold when we're surrounded by hopelessness? Jesus' birth offers both kinds of hope: hope as a tangible gift and hope as a way to live through the One born in a manger.

The lessons in this unit draw on both understandings of hope—as a gift to grasp and as a way to live. In each text, God invites us to receive the good news in the story and then live in the light of the message we discover.

God sent Jesus into a world that was familiar with hopelessness. Because God sent Jesus into such a world, we too can hear what the amazingly different message of hope sounds like.

The three Scripture texts in this unit help us hear God's hope in Jesus' birth. "The Messiah for All People" (Matthew 1:1–6, 16–17) announces Jesus' mission to all people. "Jesus—Savior—God with Us" (Matthew 1:18–25) proclaims the purpose of Christ's life—to bring salvation. "Coming to Find Jesus" (Matthew 2:1–12) invites us to the hopeful adventure of seeking Jesus. As we study these lessons, may we connect the hope we hear in Christ to the hopelessness we hear all around us.[1]

UNIT ONE. HOPE IN JESUS' BIRTH

Lesson 1	The Messiah for All People	Matthew 1:1–6, 16–17
Lesson 2	Jesus—Savior—God with Us	Matthew 1:18–25
Lesson 3	Coming to Find Jesus	Matthew 2:1–12

NOTES ————————————————————————

1. Unless otherwise indicated, all Scripture quotations in unit 1, lessons 1–3, are from the New Revised Standard Version Bible.

FOCAL TEXT
Matthew 1:1–6, 16–17

BACKGROUND
Matthew 1:1–17

MAIN IDEA
Jesus fulfills the Messianic hope of historic Judaism and is for all people everywhere.

QUESTION TO EXPLORE
How can we say Jesus is the Messiah for all people everywhere?

STUDY AIM
To explain what Jesus' genealogy means and to decide on at least one way I will participate in Jesus' mission to all people

QUICK READ
As recorded in Matthew, Jesus' family line included both Jews and Gentiles, saints and sinners, men and women, to show how God moved through history to bring the Messiah into the world for all people.

LESSON ONE
The Messiah for All People

An out-of-state college freshman, too far away from home to drive there for the weekend, promised his father that one Saturday he would visit a relative he had never met who lived only an hour's drive from his campus. Thirty minutes into the painfully polite visit, the student was planning his exit when his great-aunt brought out a family album. Sitting next to the young man, she pointed to pictures and gave colorful commentary he had never learned from his years of attending family gatherings. Suddenly his family tree grew bigger and more interesting than he had ever known. His one-time visit turned into an every-semester event that he never missed.

Perhaps we read biblical genealogies in the same way the freshman approached the visit with his great-aunt. It's something we expect to endure rather than enjoy. After all, memory verses seldom come from this section in Matthew 1. If we consider the rich histories behind those names in the genealogy, however, we might be amazed. When we attempt to discover why some names are included in Jesus' genealogy and others are not, we can become fascinated. God's family record is bigger and more interesting than we have imagined. The list of names we tend to read through quickly just might become a passage that gives us hope, one we are drawn to revisit.

MATTHEW 1:1–6, 16–17

[1]An account of the genealogy of Jesus the Messiah, the son of David, the son of Abraham. [2]Abraham was the father of Isaac, and Isaac the father of Jacob, and Jacob the father of Judah and his brothers, [3]and Judah the father of Perez and Zerah by Tamar, and Perez the father of Hezron, and Hezron the father of Aram, [4]and Aram the father of Aminadab, and Aminadab the father of Nahshon, and Nahshon the father of Salmon, [5]and Salmon the father of Boaz by Rahab, and Boaz the father of Obed by Ruth, and Obed the father of Jesse, [6]and Jesse the father of King David. And David was the father of Solomon by the wife of Uriah . . . .

·   ·   ·   ·   ·   ·   ·   ·   ·   ·   ·   ·   ·   ·   ·   ·   ·   ·   ·

[16]and Jacob the father of Joseph the husband of Mary, of whom Jesus was born, who is called the Messiah. [17]So all the generations

from Abraham to David are fourteen generations; and from David to the deportation to Babylon, fourteen generations; and from the deportation to Babylon to the Messiah, fourteen generations.

What's in a Name?

Jesus' genealogy in Matthew is more than a list of historical names, some well known and others more obscure. This family record was an invitation for faithful Jews in the writer's day to trace the connection between Jesus the Christ and their beloved ancestors of the faith. The names provided them the kind of documentation they required to see Jesus' legitimate claim to be the Messiah.

The genealogy was also a resource in which Gentiles could discover that those outside Judaism were involved in God's redemptive history. For them God's decisive act in the birth of Jesus meant far more than the arrival of the long-awaited Jewish Messiah. In this list was the hopeful assurance that they were also included in God's family, which extended far beyond the heritage of Israel.

The list of names in Jesus' family record contains surprises. While some are people whose name on the honor roll of faith seems obvious, we might expect other names to be on a different kind of list. Their stories remind us of the darker side of life, which we seldom, if ever, read to our children. The list is a testament that God worked through all kinds of men and women, those who made mistakes and committed serious sins as well as those who showed strength and courage in the faith. No one but God would include some of these names on a family tree of Jesus.

Remember that Matthew wrote of Jesus' heritage and birth knowing clearly the rest of the story. The genealogy in Matthew 1 provided embedded clues to the amazing grace of God that would be clearly seen only in the full light of Jesus' life and ministry. Matthew was prepared to write his Gospel by his transforming experience of following Jesus and knowing the power of the resurrection of the crucified Christ. He bore witness to Jesus' touching the people others thought untouchable, hearing the voices others ignored, and seeing incredible potential in people most had written off. Jesus gave hope to people who were considered hopeless.

Matthew looked back on Jesus' birth and all that had come before it through the lens of grace with which Jesus lived. Through that lens he saw and celebrated other people in the ancient past whose lives also demonstrated the reality of God's grace, who took their place in line to prepare for the one who would come, "full of grace and truth" (John 1:14).

BIBLICAL GENEALOGIES

Genealogies are records of family lineage. Such records appear in both Old and New Testaments. They are constructed in different forms and serve different family, religious, and political purposes. In Genesis genealogies are used to describe the extended families of the patriarchs, such as Noah (Gen. 10) and Abraham (Gen. 25) and to identify geographical areas where they settled. Genealogies also serve as guides to long periods of transition through the history of Israel (1 Chronicles 1—9). At times they prove the legitimacy of a person to assume a position of leadership in the worship or political life of Israel.

The New Testament provides two genealogies of the lineage of Jesus, one in Matthew 1:1–17 and another in Luke 3:23–38. Matthew traced Jesus' lineage back to Abraham to demonstrate that Jesus fulfills God's covenant with Abraham. Luke traced Jesus' line back to Adam with the apparent purpose of validating the claim that Jesus was the Son of God and Savior of the world. Both genealogies trace Jesus' heritage to David, although they do it through descendants of two different sons of David. Luke follows the line of David's son Nathan (see 2 Samuel 5:14), and Matthew traces the descendants of Solomon.

The genealogy of Matthew is more highly structured than Luke's. Matthew divided his genealogy into three sets of fourteen names. Matthew may have been using *gematria*, the practice of ancient Hebrew numerology. According to this system, words are transcribed into numerical values. Thus the Hebrew letters of the name *David* have the numerical value of fourteen. In Matthew's prominent use of the number fourteen in each of the divisions of Jesus' genealogy, some see evidence that Matthew was providing a cryptogram of the name *David*.

Matthew's Gospel spoke to a church that needed to see a bigger picture of God's love and to remember that Christ was the hope for the whole world. The church needed to grasp the wideness of God's mercy that could overcome whatever divisions they had. Where tension rose between Jews and Gentiles in the church, where the body struggled with deadly legalism on the one hand and lawlessness on the other, Matthew held up a vision of God at work to bring all people into their common hope in Jesus Christ.

Whenever we Christians are tempted to shrink the dimensions of God's love to the size of our own hearts, Matthew forces us to face the truth that in Christ there is a new reality that transcends whatever seeks to divide people. Old ways of labeling and dividing people pass away when we find ourselves in the reality of new life in Christ. We tend to want to limit God's family to the single branches we occupy or are most familiar with, but God's family is larger and more interesting than we can imagine.

Making Their Way to Jesus (1:1–6)

How would you begin the story of Jesus? Perhaps it would depend on your purpose in telling it or the particular audience you were trying to reach. Matthew was trying to reach people who took their Hebrew heritage seriously. He was aware that this audience was waiting for the promises of the Old Testament prophets to be fulfilled. He knew how the people had wrestled with issues of faith when the prophets were silent during the long inter-biblical period. Confident that the fulfillment of Israel's hope had come in Jesus, Matthew drew a family tree that placed Jesus in the long story of redemptive history. The writer shows Jesus' connection to the ways God worked in the world before Jesus' birth in Bethlehem.

Matthew introduced Jesus as the Messiah or Christ. The Greek word *christos* translated a term in Hebrew meaning *the anointed one*. In the history of the Hebrews the word applied to kings, priests, and prophets. It signified a person's empowerment by God to perform a sacred task on behalf of God's people. Through the centuries the word came to have special meaning as the people looked forward to the one who would finally come to deliver Israel and fulfill God's promise.

Matthew pointed to Jesus as "the son of David, the son of Abraham." The term "son of" meant *descended from* and could also refer to one's immediate parent. The idea that Jesus would descend from David was dominant in first-century Judaism. Matthew cited Jesus' legal descent from David and through David from Abraham. Matthew linked Jesus with the covenant God made with Abraham. In it God promised to bless Abraham and his descendants, but also declared that through them all the families of the earth would be blessed (see Genesis 12:1–3). Matthew confirmed Jesus as the One who fulfilled God's promise to Israel. He also proclaimed that the challenge given to Abraham to bless the world would be carried out through Jesus.

These verses include the mention of four women: Tamar, Rahab, Ruth, and "the wife of Uriah." This inclusion of four mothers is remarkable, because Jewish genealogies never included mothers, tracing descent instead through the father.

Readers of this Gospel would have been surprised to see women on this list at all. They would have been shocked at the women Matthew chose and the ones he skipped. Think of it—Matthew did not include such women as Sarah, Rebekah, and Rachel. Rather he mentioned mothers who had questionable lifestyles and hard lives. Too, Rahab and Ruth were non-Israelite. Some scholars think Tamar may have been as well. The wife of Uriah was married to a non-Israelite, which meant she would share Gentile status, too, according to later rabbinic law. Consider the life of each of these women.

Tamar experienced life at its worst. When her husband died, Tamar was mistreated by the men in the family, who would not care for her according to the provisions of the law. Taking matters into her own hands, she used deceptive means to force her father-in-law to take responsibility. Judah acknowledged she was right, saying: "She is more righteous than I" (Gen. 38:26). By Tamar's wiles the law was followed, and the promise of the covenant was kept alive. Her motherhood was the means by which God sustained the covenant with Israel. She was a survivor, and God was present with her.

Rahab, a prostitute, hid two Israelite spies from the king of Jericho and secured safety for her family (see Joshua 2). Her inclusion in Matthew's roll call of faith is a reminder that people far from perfect can experience the grace of God. They can also become the means by which God's grace comes to others.

Ruth's inclusion in Jesus' genealogy is a tribute to love's resiliency (see the Book of Ruth). Like Tamar and Rahab, Ruth had a rough life. A Moabite, she faced the prejudice against an interracial marriage. Ruth married into a family of Israelites who were in her native Moab because there was a famine in Israel. Then Ruth's husband died. When Ruth met and married Boaz, her new mother-in-law was Rahab. Ruth and Boaz had a son, Obed, who was the grandfather of King David. So, like Tamar and Rahab, Ruth was an ancestor of Jesus.

Matthew did not refer to Uriah's wife, Bathsheba, by name. Yet, by mentioning but not naming her, Matthew reminded his readers of the wrong David committed against her and her husband Uriah, leading to his death (see 2 Samuel 11). Even through the terse language of a formal genealogy, Matthew made clear that God used the lives of imperfect people to continue the work of grace in the world. God continues to work in such ways.

Only God Can Make a Tree (1:16–17)

Only God can make a sycamore, redwood, or live oak. In a similar way, only God could create the kind of family tree for Jesus that reaches back

---

WHAT WOULD HAPPEN IN YOUR CHURCH?

The son of a prominent physician lived in rebellion against his parents and the church in which he had grown up. Drug abuse and other self-destructive behavior marked his life. He married a young woman who was deeply involved in the same kind of lifestyle. She had no background in church life. However, through the invitation of her new mother-in-law, she began to attend worship.

One Sunday the young woman made a profession of faith. Her face reflected the rough life she had led, and her manner revealed that she felt out of place in the church setting. But when the young woman stood before the congregation, her mother-in-law quietly moved from her pew to stand beside her with her arm around her. The minister wondered: *Will the people ever accept her? Will she be able to discover her gifts for service here? How will she make a difference?*

What would happen in *your* church?

to Abraham and includes many branches for people whom others would not include. The names in Matthew's genealogy make it clear that God did not use people as stewards of the covenant because they had earned their roles through perfect lives. The record includes those whose experiences reflected their radical need of God's grace. The family record includes simple people of authentic faith as well as people of power and privilege. The line of redemption was carried not only through palaces but through the homes of the humble.

Matthew formed this genealogy into three sections of fourteen generations. Each section represented a significant period of Israel's history. The first was the era from God's promise to Abraham to the high point in the kingdom of David (Matthew 1:1–6). The second reflected the time from the decline from a united monarchy through the divided kingdom to the Babylonian Exile (Matt. 1:7–11). The third traced the redemptive line through the post-exilic period until the birth of Jesus (1:12–16). In each of these eras God was at work, in times of prosperity as well as decline, in times of faithfulness as well as unfaithfulness.

The climax of this genealogy of grace comes in an unexpected way. In straightforward and dignified words Matthew spoke of Jacob "the father of Joseph the husband of Mary, of whom Jesus was born, who is called the Messiah" (1:16). The words vary from the formula used to cite all the previous people in the genealogy. Consistent with Matthew's emphasis in 1:18–23 on the virginal conception of Jesus, Matthew avoided saying Joseph was the father of Jesus, even though Matthew was tracing the legal ancestry of Jesus through Joseph's line. In marrying Mary despite her pregnancy, Joseph assumed the legal status of Jesus' father.

Throughout the Gospels, Mary, the mother of Jesus, demonstrated her humble acceptance of the role she was asked to play in the drama of redemption. She pondered the deep meaning of all that had happened to her (Luke 2:19). She must have known unique joy in being the one who brought the Messiah into the world. She also would know the pain and sorrow of seeing his inclusive love rejected and crucified in a world of small hearts and sinful souls.

Implications and Actions

If the people in Jesus' genealogy showed up today, we might think that some of them did not belong in the church. We need to remember that God is at work in people's lives in ways that serve a purpose only God can see. Because this is true, our job is simpler. We are to share the love of God that we know through Christ with everyone. We will never meet anyone who does not need Jesus.

Our job is not to draw lines of exclusion. Rather it is to imagine God at work in the lives of people who are different from ourselves. These people may be crucial to the work of God's kingdom.

QUESTIONS

1. Why is it difficult to share the gospel and church life with people who are different from ourselves?

2. What are specific steps you or your group can take to encourage community rather than division?

3. What do you find hopeful about the people in Jesus' family tree?

4. Can you relate an experience in which you have seen the spirit of Christ unite a divided people?

5. What stirs the church to move towards Christ's mission in the world? Can you think of specific actions that may offer a congregation practical ways to express Christ's inclusive love?

FOCAL TEXT
Matthew 1:18–25

BACKGROUND
Matthew 1:18–25

MAIN IDEA
Jesus, who is God with us,
came to bring salvation.

QUESTION TO EXPLORE
What does Jesus' birth mean?

STUDY AIM
To explain the meaning of
Jesus' birth and to testify of
how it speaks to me personally

QUICK READ
We all need salvation that we
cannot achieve or produce
on our own. Jesus is the One
whom God sent to save us.

LESSON TWO
Jesus—Savior— God with Us

Wide awake in a darkened hospital room, I considered the past few months. After questioning whether we could even have a baby, we had learned that the parsonage would be containing a nursery after all. Our joyful congregation excelled at sharing our jubilation and goofiness over the positive pregnancy test. Then, that morning at church something wasn't right. We went to the hospital "just in case." The bleeding became more frequent; and I was admitted, holding tightly to the hope that everything would be just fine. Sometime in the middle of the night, our fervent prayers of *God, let this be OK*, instinctively became, *God, be with us*. When confronted with the reality I didn't want to accept, God's grace surrounded us and kept us afloat during a time of overwhelming disappointment and loss. In the ordeal of a miscarriage, we knew God's presence.

When we go through difficult days or dark nights of the soul, when problems seem bigger than we are, we instinctively long for quick solutions. We seek an easy way out or a fix for whatever trouble we face. But sometimes in the middle of our struggles, we realize that what we most want is God's saving presence with us. Whether we are caught in the consequences of our sin or someone else's, or some disaster that has no reasonable explanation, what we most need is God's saving grace.

Joseph's story in Matthew 1 is a testimony to the power of God's presence that comes in those times when nothing else can save us. Imagine responsible Joseph caught in a situation he would never have dreamed of. Yet, there he was—caught in it and dreaming of it. He prayed for a way out, for the best solution to what appeared to him to be a terrible situation. He could see no choice before him that was good. His prayers became an experience of God's presence with him, through the baby he would help deliver to the world.

MATTHEW 1:18–25

[18]Now the birth of Jesus the Messiah took place in this way. When his mother Mary had been engaged to Joseph, but before they lived together, she was found to be with child from the Holy Spirit. [19]Her husband Joseph, being a righteous man and unwilling to expose her to public disgrace, planned to dismiss her quietly. [20]But just when he had resolved to do this, an angel of the Lord appeared to him in a dream and said, "Joseph, son of David, do

not be afraid to take Mary as your wife, for the child conceived in her is from the Holy Spirit. [21]She will bear a son, and you are to name him Jesus, for he will save his people from their sins." [22]All this took place to fulfill what had been spoken by the Lord through the prophet: [23]"Look, the virgin shall conceive and bear a son, and they shall name him Emmanuel," which means, "God is with us." [24]When Joseph awoke from sleep, he did as the angel of the Lord commanded him; he took her as his wife, [25]but had no marital relations with her until she had borne a son; and he named him Jesus.

An Agonizing Change of Plans (1:18–19)

First-century Jewish marriage procedures had little in common with our practices today, which can even include proposals offered during time-outs on stadium jumbotrons. In Mary and Joseph's day, fathers made the engagement. The couple may have known each other since they were children, or they may have met only after being matched.

Betrothal was the next step in the process. Before the betrothal ceremony, which involved the couple, their parents, and witnesses, the bride-to-be could break the engagement. Once betrothed, however, a couple was legally bound, and only divorce could break their commitment. This stage of the process lasted one year, during which couples were considered legally married without living together or having sexual relations.

In the final stage of the procedure the couple married. The groom moved the bride from her father's house to his own, and a party began. Joseph and Mary were in the second stage of this marriage process, betrothal, when she became pregnant.

Scripture does not record a single word that Joseph said, but he must have been heartbroken when he heard the unexpected and unwelcome news. If Joseph were an organized, exact, logical, practical carpenter, having his well-ordered universe fall apart with no seeming possibility of putting it back together again would be especially difficult. He was a "righteous man," which meant he was committed to keeping the law.

In this circumstance the law clearly detailed what he was required to do. The only logical assumption that Joseph and anyone else could have made was that Mary had been unfaithful to him and to the requirements of her commitment to betrothal. According to Deuteronomy 22, the severe punishment that was to be carried out for such an offense was death by stoning (see Deuteronomy 22:13–21). Later developments in the interpretation of the law appear to have provided Joseph with less radical alternatives, which nevertheless seemed undesirable to him.

Joseph was a righteous man, but he was also a compassionate man. He cared for Mary. He could not treat this matter lightly, and neither would he act vindictively. He demonstrates the struggle of a soul trying to be faithful. When a person has both convictions about principles and compassion for people, he or she often faces painful choices. At times neither side of a decision seems to be totally good. Joseph could not figure out how to move through this dilemma in a way that would settle his soul. He needed saving.

The One Who Will Save You (1:20–23)

Have you ever made a major decision, perhaps tentatively, hoping that as you moved forward to implement it you could find peace and feel better about it? Yet, instead of the clouds clearing and the sunshine breaking through, your skies became murkier and more threatening. Joseph had such an experience. He had decided to divorce Mary, but not in a way that would bring her public disgrace. He would do so quietly and privately, but the decision would not quiet the turmoil in his spirit.

Then, Joseph had a dream, and in it an angel appeared with a message from God that was both reassuring and demanding. Dreams and angelic visitations had been part of the story of God's people through the ages, but Joseph had not expected such divine revelation to solve his present dilemma. The first words of angels in the Scriptures often seemed to be, "Do not be afraid"! The presence of angels often brought a response of fear before it brought an experience of calmness. The angel said to Joseph exactly what the angel Gabriel said to Mary in Luke's account of the annunciation of the birth of Jesus, "Do not be afraid!" (Luke 1:30).

The angelic assurance that came to Joseph affirmed that what was happening to Mary and him was in reality the act of God. The angel

THE POWER IN A NAME

In the biblical culture, names carried greater significance than they do in our own. A name revealed the character or essence of a person. It conveyed something about that person's abilities and functions. The process of naming a person, therefore, was taken quite seriously.

New parents today may search for a unique name or try to find one that sounds right in combination with their last name or in relation to the names of their siblings. They may consult lists of potential names for boys and girls or follow the trends of names that are currently most popular.

The names and titles given to Jesus during his ministry and following his resurrection provide insight into his nature and mission. In the study passage Matthew cited three of these significant names and titles—*Jesus, Messiah,* and *Emmanuel.*

Jesus was the name by which he was known throughout his life and ministry. As the Greek form of the Hebrew name *Joshua,* it meant *Yahweh is salvation.* Some translate it in the form of a prayer, *O Lord, save.*

Messiah was a Hebrew term meaning *anointed one.* Translated by the Greek word *christos,* it was applied to kings, priests, and prophets. They were seen as chosen and enabled by God to perform vital tasks for God's people. It came to have special significance to designate the promised one who would come to save Israel and thus was applied to Jesus.

Emmanuel was a personal Hebrew name meaning *God with us.* Used in Isaiah 7:14, the name was applied to Jesus by the angel in Joseph's dream.

brought the message that God was doing something momentous in their lives. This momentous act was the fulfillment of a long-awaited promise to God's people. It was the movement of the living God in history to bring hope and save the people from their sins. The angel encouraged the silent Joseph, saying in effect: *Don't hesitate to get married. Your confidence in and compassion for Mary are well-founded. The Spirit made Mary pregnant. She will give birth to a son; and when she does, you will name him "Jesus." His name itself will mean "God saves." God is acting to save his people from their sins.* Jesus' name would in itself let everyone know not only who he was, but also what he was to do.

The message of the angel reminded Joseph that what was happening fulfilled a prophetic word of hope. Isaiah had said: "Look, the virgin shall conceive and bear a son, and they shall name him Emmanuel" (Matthew 1:23; see Isaiah 7:14). Even if Joseph had known and remembered this word, he had not previously applied it to his situation. Through the word of the prophet, Joseph saw that he was not abandoned by God; instead, God was coming near. God was coming to be with his people in a new way. A baby was going to be born.

Talk about a change in perspective! Joseph had thought that the baby was his *problem.* Now he heard that the baby would be his *solution*—and not his alone. The baby would be the Savior of all God's people.

The solutions to our most difficult problems frequently begin when we change our perspective on them. We need to first ask: *God, do you see this as I'm seeing it? Am I missing what is really going on here? Am I too close to the pain to see the promise of your presence?* As in all true communion with God, Joseph discovered he was not alone. With the presence and promise of God, he could face whatever would come from all those around him who would never be able to understand.

When we gain God's perspective on our lives, our prayers often change. What we thought was our greatest need may recede. What we had not recognized comes to the forefront of our concern. In the promise of the birth of Jesus, even in his name itself, the angelic word focused on our primary need. "He will save his people from their sins" (Matt. 1:21). The

WHAT WOULD JESUS DO—WITH YOU?

When Emmanuel, God with us, became part of Joseph's life, Joseph found strength to love and live in remarkable ways. When Emmanuel, God with us, becomes part of our lives, we find strength to

- Love faithfully
- Follow the dreams God gives us
- Take the road less traveled
- Do the hard work of caring for those who need our care

Jews in the first century expected that the Messiah would deliver Israel from the rule of those who had oppressed her. The Messiah would come as an instrument of God's judgment, and the target of this judgment would be on other nations because of their sins against God's people.

Jesus' mission as Messiah would be focused on Israel herself. He would concentrate on delivering the people from their sins. How easy it had been for them to think their primary difficulty could be blamed on the sins of others. If only we could be released from this bondage, they thought, we could come into our own. If only God punished others, we could be given our rightful place.

In Jesus, God was coming near to the people, but it was not to change their circumstances as much as to change *them*. Many people who were looking for Messiah could never accept Jesus as Emmanuel, *God with us*, because he did not fit their preconception of what Messiah was to do. They resisted seeing themselves as the problem. They did not have the honesty to look deep into their own lives or the courage to confess the sin they saw there.

Faithful to His Dream (1:24–25)

For many of us, dreams are easily forgotten when we awaken. Too, dreams are subject to all kinds of interpretation. Even what we think for a moment to be the whisper of an angel can easily be reinterpreted. After waking from his dream, Joseph could have abandoned the angel's risky counsel to follow a more sensible course, such as following through on his decision to leave Mary. But Joseph decided to take a huge risk based solely on a dream. When faced with the choice of doing what seemed reasonable or taking a big chance, Joseph embraced the unexpected.

Joseph did not consider the message from the angel as merely an interesting suggestion to be considered. He accepted it as a word from God to be believed and a command to be obeyed.

The supporting role Joseph received in the drama of redemption was difficult to play. In accepting his role and beginning to play it, Joseph demonstrated a great capacity for faith. He believed God had spoken to him. He dared to believe the seemingly ridiculous idea that the living God would work the plan to redeem humankind through a baby born to a simple peasant girl and a carpenter from Nazareth.

Joseph also demonstrated a remarkable capacity for courage. To join God in this redemptive movement in the world meant experiencing crisis and intense opposition. From the very beginning of Jesus' story this proved to be true. Joseph and Mary faced the gossip of those in Nazareth who wanted to think the worst of Mary. They experienced the hatred of Herod, who would destroy anything he thought threatened his power. Their roles required them to experience the pain of identifying with the loving God in a hostile world.

Implications and Actions

Each of us needs the assurance that God is with us and that God has come to save. Whether we are parents who face agonizing disappointment in the loss of an expected baby or parents-to-be who face bewilderment and shame in the birth of an unexpected baby, we need the assurance that God is with us. Whether we feel abandoned by God in circumstances over which we have no control or caught in the consequences of our own sinful choices, we need more than anything to know the saving presence of the loving God. To live in such confidence is to become a survivor or overcomer rather than a victim in any circumstance.

The focus of Matthew's Gospel is the proclamation that the saving presence of God has come to us in the person of Jesus, the Christ. Joseph provides a model of faith and courage for anyone who dares to claim this incredible promise of hope. In the beginning of the Gospel the assurance is proclaimed in the name "Emmanuel." Throughout the life and ministry of Jesus the empowering presence of Jesus made the decisive difference for his disciples. The final words of the risen Christ in Matthew 28:20 were "Remember, I am with you always, to the end of the age."

A follower of Jesus lives in the conviction that Jesus is with us. Even so, Jesus' saving presence in our lives is not for us alone. He is with us for others. Our lives are not to be cul-de-sacs of Jesus' saving presence, but thoroughfares to the hearts of people who need to know they are not alone.

QUESTIONS

1. How would you describe what is means to be *saved by God* to someone who is unfamiliar with the terms we use in church?

2. How does being saved from our sins affect our lives every day?

3. How did Joseph's life change over the course of this story? What questions would you like to ask this man who never said a word that is recorded in Scripture?

4. What does the story of Mary and Joseph show us about God's love?

5. When have you experienced most intensely the need to be saved?

FOCAL TEXT
Matthew 2:1–12

BACKGROUND
Matthew 2

MAIN IDEA

The Wise Men's seeking and worshiping Jesus signifies that Jesus is for all people and calls us to reach out to all people for Jesus' sake.

QUESTION TO EXPLORE

What are we doing about the New Testament truth that Jesus is for all people?

STUDY AIM

To identify ways I will participate in Jesus' mission for reaching the people some people call "foreigners"

QUICK READ

Jesus' birth is God's gift for all people, but people respond to the event differently. Some, like the Wise Men, seek Jesus sincerely and worship him gratefully; others, like Herod, see Jesus as a threat and reject God's gift.

LESSON THREE
Coming to Find Jesus

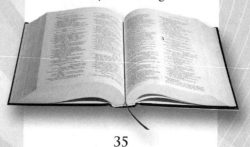

One Epiphany Sunday, when our class was studying the story of the Wise Men seeking Jesus, I passed out paper and pens and asked each member to respond to this question: "What are you seeking at this time in your life?" Several members didn't look thrilled with the assignment, especially when I explained we were going to do what writing teachers call *freewriting*.

"Just keep your pen moving for the next ten minutes," I said. "Don't stop, and see what flows." I quickly added that if writing wasn't their forte, they could make a list of what they might be seeking in the New Year. To my surprise, everyone started writing feverishly, even the less than thrilled. I even hesitated to call *time*.

When we shared responses, people spoke about seeking answers, boldness, courage, and ways to let go of fear. As we studied the story of the Wise Men, the group drew parallels between those ancient travelers and our own journeys to grow in our faith. Maybe the exercise worked because New Year's resolutions were still on our minds. Maybe there were more closet poets in our group than we realized. Or perhaps the pens kept flowing because seeking is a crucial part of our lives. We may not label ourselves *seekers*, but Christians seek to grow in Christ, label or not.

The search for what is true is continuous and not confined to any one stage of life. The desire to discover the source of grace cannot be contained in any demographic or region of the world. God nurtures the adventure of seeking in us so that we will discover more of who God is and, as a result, more of who we can become.

MATTHEW 2:1–12

¹In the time of King Herod, after Jesus was born in Bethlehem of Judea, wise men from the East came to Jerusalem, ²asking, "Where is the child who has been born king of the Jews? For we observed his star at its rising, and have come to pay him homage." ³When King Herod heard this, he was frightened, and all Jerusalem with him; ⁴and calling together all the chief priests and scribes of the people, he inquired of them where the Messiah was to be born. ⁵They told him, "In Bethlehem of Judea; for so it

has been written by the prophet: ⁶"And you, Bethlehem, in the land of Judah, are by no means least among the rulers of Judah; for from you shall come a ruler who is to shepherd my people Israel.' " ⁷Then Herod secretly called for the wise men and learned from them the exact time when the star had appeared. ⁸Then he sent them to Bethlehem, saying, "Go and search diligently for the child; and when you have found him, bring me word so that I may also go and pay him homage." ⁹When they had heard the king, they set out; and there, ahead of them, went the star that they had seen at its rising, until it stopped over the place where the child was. ¹⁰When they saw that the star had stopped, they were overwhelmed with joy. ¹¹On entering the house, they saw the child with Mary his mother; and they knelt down and paid him homage. Then, opening their treasure chests, they offered him gifts of gold, frankincense, and myrrh. ¹²And having been warned in a dream not to return to Herod, they left for their own country by another road.

Sincere Seekers of Truth

As you read Matthew 2:1–12, notice the striking contrasts between the major characters—the Wise Men and King Herod. This story demonstrates both trust and rejection through the ways that people respond to God's gift of Jesus. The Wise Men responded as those who see what God is doing in history and want to be involved in it. Herod represents those in every age who see nothing in the providential work of God except a threat to their own self-interests. The Wise Men symbolize the diversity of people beyond the boundaries of Israel who ultimately accept Jesus. Herod foreshadows the rejection and persecution Jesus will suffer at home from his own people.

The Wise Men, or Magi, were non-Jews, *foreigners*, but they traveled far to bring their costly gifts to the Christ child. Their identities are mysterious. They appeared for a brief but essential moment in the Christmas drama. Then they disappeared. All that we know about them comes from the meaning of the word *magi* itself and the events surrounding the infancy of Jesus. The word *magi* is Persian in origin and probably refers in the text to Babylonian astrologers. These students of the stars came to Herod searching for the meaning of the unusual heavenly phenomenon they had sighted. They determined that the unique star they discovered signified the birth of a king, but they did not know where he had been born.

Although their origins are obscure and their biographical data sketchy, the actions of the Wise Men reveal characteristics that Christians in any age emulate in their search for Jesus. The Wise Men were single-minded in their quest for truth. They were not deterred by anything or anyone in their obsession to follow the star and discover its meaning. No one knows the length of their quest or how old Jesus was when they found him. Clues in the story indicate that the child was probably less than two years old. Their commitment ultimately brought them success in their venture. When they looked to Herod for help, the chief priests and scribes helped them discover that Bethlehem in Judah would be their final destination.

The tangible gifts that the Wise Men brought to Jesus were sincere expressions of their faith in him. While the meaning of their gifts has been subject to much speculation, one thing is certain. The gifts were costly. Although unsuitable for a little child, they were fit for a king. Maybe they provided needed resources for Joseph and Mary as they fled into Egypt and faced an uncertain future. Maybe the Wise Men served the young King in ways they did not fully understand.

The latter part of the story (Matthew 2:12) shows how the Magi continued to seek God's leadership. They obeyed the instruction they received in a dream to avoid Herod on their return journey and took an alternate route. In a similar way, Christian disciples continue to seek God's leading in our daily lives, being open to God's leading in ways we did not plan or expect.

An Insecure Seeker of Power

News from the Wise Men threatened Herod and "frightened" this insecure ruler (Matt. 2:3). He determined to take any steps necessary to seek out and destroy any other claimant to his throne. As ruler of the Jews under Rome from approximately 37 B.C. until his death in 4 B.C., he provided relative stability for the people of Israel. He was a cruel man,

THE TRADITION OF THE MAGI

We read the story of the Magi through the lens of tradition that has accumulated for centuries. While the information about them in the text is actually sparse, time has filled in the blanks with speculation and tradition that seems like fact for many readers. For example, we assume that the number of Magi was three, but this idea simply developed from the fact there were three gifts presented to Jesus. We assume they were kings, but there is no reference to this in Matthew's text. We often assume they arrived at the manger immediately after the shepherds, but the Scripture text indicates differently. This idea has been perpetuated in traditional Christmas pageants and on Christmas cards throughout history. The biblical story indicates that they arrived sometime after the birth of Jesus, when the family had moved from the stable to a house.

The Magi were mysterious in their origin and destiny. Later tradition gave them names. By 600 A.D. legend had named them Caspar, Melchior, and Balthasar.

however, who took drastic action to keep or enhance his power. When Herod was frightened or disturbed, the people were likewise fearful and insecure. When Herod was unhappy, everyone was unhappy, because they knew the consequences of his rage.

Although Herod was a Jew by birth, he did not exemplify the tenets of Judaism or its moral ideals during his reign. He took whatever path led to power, disregarding and sacrificing moral principle and bringing harm to others. Herod symbolizes how far people will go to preserve their self-interest. When the Magi asked him where the new king of the Jews would be born, Herod pretended to share their noble desires to find him in order to worship him. Like Herod, people in every age may profess interest in worshiping the Christ, when in reality this is their pretense rather than their true desire.

The background text for today's passage describes the extent of Herod's obsessive madness. The Magi did not return with information about the location of the Christ child, as Herod instructed them to do. He reacted in rage and ordered the slaughter of all children in and around Bethlehem who were under two years old (2:16–18).

Then Joseph responded to a dream in which he heard a warning from an angel of the Lord. Joseph took Mary and Jesus and fled in the night to the safety of Egypt until the danger had passed. Imagine the sense of relief Joseph must have felt when he heard the reassuring words of the angel of the Lord: "Those who were seeking the child's life are dead" (2:20).

Those who hear of Jesus respond to him in varied ways. Some like the Magi eagerly seek him and offer their love. Others like Herod understand that his presence will change their lives. They reject this threat with open hostility or silent apathy. In our kind of world, we may wonder whether God's gift of Jesus is rejected more than received. God assures us, as God assured those in every age, that the child will survive and overcome long after those who oppose him have become mere footnotes in history.

An Enduring Symbol of Hope

As students of the stars, the Magi searched the heavens for new phenomena. They believed that astrological happenings were related to events in human history. The Magi related their observation of an unusual sighting in the sky to the birth of a king. People in the ancient world widely believed that the birth of an important person would be marked by the appearance of a special star or astrological display.

THE UNIVERSAL SAVIOR

Matthew presents Jesus not only as the Messiah of Israel but also as Savior *of the world*. The story of the Magi gives some of the first clues that the impact of Jesus' birth would reach far beyond Israel. The final words of Jesus in Matthew 28:19–20 point to the universal mission of Jesus' followers.

The words of the Old Testament prophets can stretch our minds and hearts to see that God's purpose in the birth of Jesus goes far beyond providing salvation for a few to reaching all humankind with the experience of saving grace. Read the following Scriptures: Micah 5:2–5; Isaiah 2:1–4; Isaiah 60:1–6.

When the Magi came to Jerusalem, they asked where the new king had been born. They explained the reason for their request: "For we observed his star at its rising" (2:2). This translation is clearer and more accurate than the traditional version that refers to "his star in the east" (KJV). The word does not indicate that the star was in the eastern sky or that they were in the east when they saw it. The term refers to the Magi's observation of the beginning of this unique event in the heavens. These conscientious scanners of night skies saw Jesus' natal star at the time of its first rising.

The Magi saw the star in their own homeland. They associated their observation with the widespread speculation that a king of the Jews would be born. They came to Jerusalem to validate their conviction that such a king would be born there. Note that the star itself is not mentioned as a guide for them on their journey to Jerusalem. They evidently knew the way. After consulting with Herod and the interpreters of the law and the prophets, they learned about the prophet Micah's prediction that a shepherd king would come from the little town of Bethlehem. This was the city of David, a most appropriate place for the birth of the Son of David who was the long-expected Messiah. When the Magi resumed their journey to Bethlehem, the star again appeared, moving before them and guiding them to the place the young child was staying. There it stopped.

The amazing event brings inevitable questions to readers today. How does a star move in such an exceptional way? Are there other examples of such phenomena? Were the Magi the only people who were able to see the star? If others saw it, was there some public excitement and interest? The biblical account does not address all the questions that inquiring minds might want to know. No attempt to explain this mysterious heavenly phenomenon historically or scientifically has been successful. The story focuses less on the spectacular heavenly phenomenon and more on those who followed the star and the one to whom it led. For them the star was a visible symbol of God's action in history, providing the guidance they needed in their lives. The Magi saw the star as a sign of God's providential preparation of a new era of truth for those who were open to receive it.

The star in the story of the birth of Jesus continues to endure as a symbol of hope for a world in despair. To those needing direction and assurance it declares that in Jesus God has acted to bring salvation *to the world.* The star of hope, which guided the Magi long ago, through the centuries has led people from everywhere to the baby of Bethlehem, to whom grateful souls still bring their gifts of love.

Implications and Actions

The Magi reflect our human capacity to search for knowledge we do not yet have and wisdom that comes only from beyond ourselves. Their dramatic story reminds us that we all need stars of hope to guide us. We all take journeys that lead us to discover God's grace. Our life journey does not end in Bethlehem. It only begins there. We kneel before the gift of grace we receive in Christ. Then we rise to begin following Jesus, wherever he leads us. In his company we discover the meaningful life we could never find on our own.

Do we have the courage to seek this wisdom that comes in following Jesus? Are we willing to give up our sense of control and go where Christ leads us? The Magi wanted to see Jesus more than they wanted to keep their treasures or play it safe by studying stars from afar. They wanted to seek after God more than they feared the difficulties of the journey. The Magi embraced the quest, and on the way discovered they were not alone. Indeed, the Magi remind us that the way is open for us and all people to seek Christ.

QUESTIONS

1. What are you seeking at this time in your life?

2. What characteristics of the Magi do you see in yourself? What do you need to learn from their story?

3. How do you stay open to God's leading in your life?

4. What gifts do you offer Jesus?

5. While you may not identify with Herod, have you ever felt
    threatened by the truth that Christ will change our lives?
    How do you respond to that fear?

6. What does the likelihood that the Magi were non-Jews, *foreigners*,
    suggest to you?

Hope in Jesus' Ministry

Studying beginnings is important. Grasping where we came from can help us understand where we are now.

This thought applies to the life of Jesus. In this unit we discover how Jesus came on the scene as a dynamic teacher, preacher, and healer. John the Baptist had laid the foundation (see Matthew 3). He preached repentance, warning that God was about to break into the world in a dramatic way called the kingdom of God (or heaven). John immersed in the Jordan River people who repented.

One day John's cousin, Jesus, came to be baptized. After initial resistance, John agreed to baptize him. As Jesus came out of the water, the Holy Spirit descended on him like a dove, and a voice from heaven expressed God's approval.

Immediately after, the Spirit impelled Jesus into the wilderness, a wild and lonely place. There Jesus fasted and meditated forty days. Satan then came to Jesus and tried him with three recorded temptations. Jesus answered the devil with scriptural quotes and so fixed his purpose of obedience to God.

Following Herod's arrest of John, Jesus picked up where John left off. Jesus preached, taught, and healed. Crowds followed him. From those crowds Jesus called out disciples to form his inner circle.

Let us now look at these events to see what they can tell us about how we should live as Jesus' followers. Pray for the Spirit's leadership in your life as you consider these lessons.[1]

UNIT TWO. HOPE IN JESUS' MINISTRY

NOTES

1. Unless otherwise indicated, all Scripture quotations in unit 2, lessons 4–5, are from the New International Version.

BACKGROUND
Matthew 3:1—4:11

MAIN IDEA
Jesus' overcoming temptation shows that in his ministry he would be fully faithful to God's way rather than following the way of worldly selfishness.

QUESTION TO EXPLORE
How are you being tempted today?

STUDY AIM
To identify ways in which Jesus' temptations can be compared to mine and determine how I can overcome temptation as Jesus did

QUICK READ
Jesus overcame Satan's temptations by responding with Scripture and in so doing decided to be the kind of Messiah God wanted him to be.

LESSON FOUR
Fully Faithful to God's Way

One summer at youth camp, a senior girl confided in me her struggle with temptation. She wanted to live as a Christian, but she found herself often failing. She felt quite discouraged in her struggle. I suggested she read Paul's confession on the subject at the end of Romans 7. She came back later, expressing amazement that such a dynamic missionary could have had similar struggles.

Of course, you and I also share those battles with temptation. My prayer is that we can all gain strength from studying how Jesus dealt with temptation and find ways to apply his way to our own dealings with Satan. This lesson focuses on Jesus' wrestling with obedience to God as the Messiah and his struggle to determine what kind of Messiah to be.

MATTHEW 4:1–11

[1]Then Jesus was led by the Spirit into the desert to be tempted by the devil. [2]After fasting forty days and forty nights, he was hungry. [3]The tempter came to him and said, "If you are the Son of God, tell these stones to become bread." [4]Jesus answered, "It is written: 'Man does not live on bread alone, but on every word that comes from the mouth of God.'" [5]Then the devil took him to the holy city and had him stand on the highest point of the temple. [6]"If you are the Son of God," he said, "throw yourself down. For it is written: "'He will command his angels concerning you, and they will lift you up in their hands, so that you will not strike your foot against a stone.'" [7]Jesus answered him, "It is also written: 'Do not put the Lord your God to the test.'" [8]Again, the devil took him to a very high mountain and showed him all the kingdoms of the world and their splendor. [9]"All this I will give you," he said, "if you will bow down and worship me." [10]Jesus said to him, "Away from me, Satan! For it is written: 'Worship the Lord your God, and serve him only.'" [11]Then the devil left him, and angels came and attended him.

Background: John Baptizes Jesus (3:1–17)

A strange-looking man dressed in animal skins appeared in the country-side around the Jordan River. He preached a powerful message, warning that God was about to break into his world in a powerful way. People needed to prepare for this event by changing their way of living.

Many people went to hear this man's dynamic message. When they responded, he—John the Baptist—immersed them in the waters of the Jordan.

Jesus came to be baptized also. John felt Jesus to be his superior. Why should the lesser baptize the greater? But Jesus answered that it was God's will. Indeed, a voice from heaven spoke as Jesus rose from the water. The voice said, "This is my Son, whom I love; with him I am well pleased" (Matthew 3:17).

Why was Jesus baptized? He had no sins for which to repent. However, Jesus set us an example and also identified himself with John the Baptist's movement. Too, the immersion marked his public commitment to do the work of the Messiah.

The First Temptation: Making Bread (4:1–4)

After Jesus was baptized, the Holy Spirit led him into the desert wilderness to reflect on what it meant to be the Messiah. Most Jews expected a military leader. The Essenes in Qumran looked also for a second messiah, an anointed priest. Satan attacked Jesus with temptations to use spectacular shortcuts to win popular approval rather than the difficult road leading to a cross.

Note that the Spirit led Jesus into temptation. We often have a wishy-washy view of God, picturing God to be like a heavenly grandparent who never gives anything but sweets and lets us get away with whatever we want. On the contrary, God wanted his Son to face the adversary from the beginning. The kinds of temptations Jesus faced would crop up again and again in his life and ministry. By facing these temptations at the very beginning, Jesus made basic decisions about his ministry.

Jesus began this period with a fast. Satan knew Jesus was hungry. Some of the stones in the area may have resembled loaves of bread. So the devil played on Jesus' hunger, as he preys on our weaknesses, suggesting that Jesus turn the stones to bread. If Jesus were the Son of God, why should he depend on getting food from human sources? Note that Matthew strongly emphasizes Jesus' identity as Son of God, using the term frequently.

Satan was also proposing that Jesus use his Messianic powers to become popular by feeding people. But had Jesus done so, the motive would have been for Jesus' own benefit—the approval of the people. Later Jesus would indeed feed crowds of people, but for *their* benefit. Jesus rejected the idea of becoming a leader simply by catering to people's physical needs. Neither would Jesus use divine power to meet his own needs.

Three times Jesus answered Satan from Scripture, each time from the Book of Deuteronomy. Jesus' responses show the value he placed on Scripture. We would do well to seek to evaluate and support our own thoughts and actions by saturating our minds with Scripture.

At this point Jesus' quote indicated that we do "not live on bread alone" (Matt. 4:4). Rather, the real source of life is spiritual—"every word that comes from the mouth of God" (4:4, from Deuteronomy 8:3). Jesus kept his mind fixed on spiritual, not physical reality.

The Second Temptation: A Spectacular Leap (4:5–7)

Next, Satan placed Jesus at some point atop the Jerusalem temple. Since the temple had neither steeple nor tower, we're not sure where that point was. Perhaps Jesus looked down from atop one of the colonnades or porches at the people below. Neither do we know for sure whether Satan actually moved Jesus physically to the temple or whether the event happened in a vision. Whichever way, the temptation was real.

TEMPTATION

The Greek word lying behind "tempted" (Matt. 4:1) can also mean *tested*. The word lies behind our word *pirates*, who were certainly trials for seafarers. In James the word is used to mean both temptation and trial (James 1:12–13). The two ideas are linked. Not all trials are temptations, except as they put pressure on us that may weaken us to the devil's allurements. But every temptation is also a trial, a test.

If you succeed in obeying God as you face temptation, you emerge stronger than before. If you fail, you need to seek forgiveness and strengthening for your Christian life.

Again Satan reminded Jesus that Scripture promises God will look after his Chosen One. So why not make use of that fact, leap from the top of the temple, and emerge unhurt to crowds of cheering admirers? But Jesus pointed to another verse that says not to tempt, or "test," God (Deut. 6:16). Jumping off a high place would indeed be pushing God to the limit. Further, tempting God's Son was the same as tempting God himself. Jesus thus declared he would not use spectacular displays to draw attention to himself. People would follow him for spiritual purposes, not sensationalism.

Two dangers show up for us here. The first danger is that we interpret Scripture to our own advantage. For example, consider the statement "I am with you always" (Matt. 28:20). It's certainly true that Jesus is with us always. In Matthew 28:20, though, the verse is linked to the missionary command. Indeed, the promises of God's presence generally relate to people on mission for him. Certainly God is with us all the time. But the promises of God's special presence and care have special application when people are seeking to fulfill God's call for their lives.

The second danger is that we equate temptation only with certain actions we label as sins. Temptation certainly includes these, but let us not forget that sins include sins of omission as well of commission, including making major life choices without seeking God's will. We may feel quite guilty after lying to someone, but our conscience may not trouble us when we fail to help another person. Too, do we consider temptation to be present as we decide whether to take one job over another or ponder our response to challenging situations in the workplace? Jesus' first two temptations involved the best way to serve God's purpose.

The Third Temptation: Worship Satan (4:8–11)

Finally, the devil revealed his ultimate goal. He sought for the Messiah to change sides, from serving God to serving Satan. From a mountaintop the devil showed Jesus all the kingdoms of the world. Satan claimed to own them and have the power to choose their rulers. Do you think Satan had the power to fulfill his promise to Jesus? Whatever the answer, Satan demanded that Jesus worship him, not God. If the Messiah would do that, Satan would immediately make him ruler over the world. For this

---

FACING TEMPTATION

- Recognize it
- Pray for God's help in dealing with it
- Recall Scripture that applies to it
- Anticipate that it will recur
- Decide ahead of time to resist it
- Find a confidential friend you trust to help you deal with it

---

the devil quoted no Scripture as he had done in the previous temptation. Indeed, there was none he could quote.

But Jesus shot back another verse from Deuteronomy. "Worship the Lord, your God, and serve Him only" (Matt. 4:10; Deut. 6:13). He had no intention of changing his allegiance. The fundamental focus of the Bible, both in the Old and New Testaments, is worshiping only the one true God. See, for example, Deuteronomy 6:4, "Hear, O Israel: The LORD our God, the LORD is one. Love the LORD your God with all your heart and with all your soul and with all your strength." Jesus endorsed it as "the first and greatest commandment" (Matt. 22:37).

Note also that Jesus prefaced his quote this time with a command to Satan to leave him. And verse 11 says the devil did just that.

Implications and Applications

1. These temptations of Jesus focus on Jesus' life's work. We often limit our view of temptation to single personal acts. Yet Satan attacked Jesus at the root of his life. If Jesus had fallen for these temptations, everything else he did would have been wrong. In today's world, people change jobs, even careers, several times during their lifetimes. In wrestling with such a basic decision, affecting everything else you do, make sure you are guided by the Holy Spirit. Don't fall for the devil's temptations. The principle also applies to all our basic decisions. Involve God in all your life.

2. Jesus saturated himself with Scripture. God's word was immediately at hand. How rooted are your thoughts and decisions in biblical teachings? Do Bible teachings come easily to mind when making choices?

3. Jesus devoted forty days to consider the road ahead. We often plunge into the next phase of our lives without deeply considering our goals and their relation to God's will. Why not schedule a quiet week of vacation, or at least a weekend, to consider what to do before plunging in to your next major stage of life or your next major decision?

4. The principles in this lesson's Scriptures apply to daily enticements and sinful actions as well as to major life decisions. Getting the big choices right makes the smaller, daily temptations easier, but these daily enticements still require struggle and faith. Most of us have some besetting sins and temptations that recur. Temper, lust, fear—fill in yours here. Focus on the teachings in this passage that would lead you to greater integrity and victorious living.

QUESTIONS

1. What are the next major life-altering decisions facing you?

2. How would the temptations of Jesus relate to the choices life will require you to make?

3. What are your personal pet sins or temptations? What does Scripture teach about them? What will you have to do to tell Satan to go away?

4. The Spirit led Jesus to the wilderness. Where is God leading you?

FOCAL TEXT
Matthew 4:12–25

BACKGROUND
Matthew 4:12–25

MAIN IDEA

Jesus changed people's lives as they responded to his proclamation of the kingdom of heaven in word and deed.

QUESTION TO EXPLORE

In what ways do you yet need to respond to Jesus' ministry?

STUDY AIM

To evaluate my response to Jesus' ministry in light of the response of the people of Jesus' day and decide on how I will allow Jesus to change my life

QUICK READ

Jesus came on the scene teaching, preaching, healing, and calling disciples. People responded eagerly to his message and actions.

LESSON FIVE
The Dawning Light

As every year begins, I wonder where I'll be fifty-two weeks later. Will I be in the same town, the same house, the same job? Or will I move to who knows where? Perhaps you likewise consider your life in a special way at the beginning of a year.

We do well to look back at the past from time to time to learn how we arrived in the here and now. We also do well to look forward to where we may be going.

The world made a new start 2,000 years ago. Light shined in the darkness. A new presence came on the scene—a man called Jesus. He spoke as no one had ever spoken. He changed lives as no one had ever done. He collected a band of dedicated followers, both to learn and to carry out his mission. As you study this Scripture passage, take time to review where your life stands in light of Jesus.

MATTHEW 4:12–25

[12]When Jesus heard that John had been put in prison, he returned to Galilee. [13]Leaving Nazareth, he went and lived in Capernaum, which was by the lake in the area of Zebulun and Naphtali— [14]to fulfill what was said through the prophet Isaiah: [15]"Land of Zebulun and land of Naphtali, the way to the sea, along the Jordan, Galilee of the Gentiles— [16]the people living in darkness have seen a great light; on those living in the land of the shadow of death a light has dawned." [17]From that time on Jesus began to preach, "Repent, for the kingdom of heaven is near." [18]As Jesus was walking beside the Sea of Galilee, he saw two brothers, Simon called Peter and his brother Andrew. They were casting a net into the lake, for they were fishermen. [19]"Come, follow me," Jesus said, "and I will make you fishers of men." [20]At once they left their nets and followed him. [21]Going on from there, he saw two other brothers, James son of Zebedee and his brother John. They were in a boat with their father Zebedee, preparing their nets. Jesus called them, [22]and immediately they left the boat and their father and followed him. [23]Jesus went throughout Galilee, teaching in their synagogues, preaching the good news of the kingdom, and healing every disease and sickness among the people. [24]News about him spread all over Syria, and people brought to him all

who were ill with various diseases, those suffering severe pain, the demon-possessed, those having seizures, and the paralyzed, and he healed them. ²⁵Large crowds from Galilee, the Decapolis, Jerusalem, Judea and the region across the Jordan followed him.

Jesus' Message (4:12–17)

John the Baptist's preaching got him in trouble. Herod Antipas arrested him to stop his criticism (see Mark 6:17). At that point, Jesus moved forward with his own ministry. Jesus took up residence in Capernaum, a seaside village still within Herod's domain. Jesus' first disciples seem to have lived there or nearby. Note that Matthew saw this as fulfilling Scripture.

Matthew wrote with Jewish readers in mind. So he quoted Old Testament verses that show the fulfillment of prophecy. Isaiah predicted that the territory of Nazareth and Capernaum (the tribes of Zebulun and Naphtali) would see "a great light" (Isaiah 9:1–2). On them the "light has dawned." Many expected the Messiah to come from Jerusalem, the city of David, or at least the tribe of Judah. Matthew shows that one of the greatest prophets saw light coming out of darkness in Galilee. He also characterized the area as "Galilee of the Gentiles." The Wise Men had also come from non-Jewish territories. Matthew thus emphasized that Jesus was for the whole world.

Compare Matthew 4:17 with 3:2. Jesus began by preaching exactly the same message as John, "Repent, for the kingdom of heaven is near."

"Repent" means *to change direction*. The parallel Hebrew word in the Old Testament means literally *to turn*. The word is used of physically going one way and then changing to go another. In the New Testament, the usual word translated "repent" means *to change one's mind or purpose*. One can picture a person traveling down a road away from God, stopping, and then turning around to go back toward God. Biblical repentance is a radical change in mind, attitude, and behavior. Jesus' call was not merely to feel sorrow or guilt but to reverse one's direction of life.

Have you ever driven past the turn-off to your destination, perhaps thinking of something else? You catch yourself, turn around, and go back the direction you should have followed in the first place. That's what repentance means in the Bible.

Feeling sorry or guilty may motivate repentance, but true repentance is more than a feeling. It is a behavior. Paul explains the difference in 2 Corinthians 7:9–10. "Yet now I am happy, not because you were made sorry, but because your sorrow led you to repentance. For you became sorrowful as God intended. . . . Godly sorrow brings repentance that leads to salvation and leaves no regret, but worldly sorrow brings death."

What did John the Baptist and Jesus mean by "the kingdom of heaven"? At the very least, a kingdom implies two things: a ruler and subjects. So at a minimum the kingdom of heaven points to God (or Christ) as king and the people of God as his subjects. (The term is equivalent to the expression *the kingdom of God* elsewhere in the New Testament. Matthew was writing with a Jewish audience in mind. To avoid taking the name of the Lord in vain, the Jews avoided using the word *God* and substituted another term, such as *heaven*.)

One definition of the kingdom of heaven (or the kingdom of God) is that it is *the rule and reign of God in the hearts and lives of God's people.* Jesus proclaimed the kingdom as "near" (Matt. 4:17, NIV) or "at hand" (NASB, KJV). The word signifies the approach of something. We might compare a train coming into a station. The engine comes first, but there may be a mile or more of cars following. With the arrival of Jesus, the kingdom broke into the world. Yet Jesus taught us to pray "your kingdom come" (6:10), which means that realm is not yet fully realized. Nevertheless, Jesus preached a sense of urgency because God was about to do something new and powerful.

Calling Disciples (4:18–22)

We're used to the story in these verses, but pretend you come on it for the first time. This man strolled down the beach and saw a couple of fishermen working with their nets. The man called out like a commanding officer, *Here! After me!* As soldiers obey their superiors, so Peter and Andrew turned and followed Jesus.

Imagine a movie or television show (or perhaps your own military experience) in which a commander calls to one or more of his team:

"Smith, Jones, with me." The commander then walks out with the ones he called following. Taking the Gospel of Matthew by itself, the scene was indeed that abrupt. The writer was showing the authority of Jesus, his power to attract followers. The Gospel of John in all likelihood was written much later than the Gospel of Matthew. But John added a story that tells us that Peter and Andrew had met Jesus before, in Judea (John 1:35–51). I suspect that Jesus observed those who came to hear him and speak with him. From these people, Jesus then prayerfully selected twelve to be specially trained as a central team. Nevertheless, the call was abrupt, unexpected, and strong.

Jesus called them to a major job change. He required them to re-orient their lives. Leaving secure homes and jobs, they were to travel with him wherever he went. Note that he laid out no agenda or program. He promised no rewards. He simply said, "Come, follow me."

"Fishers of men" is a vivid term. You may be so familiar with these words that you read over them without much thought. For most who fish, fishing is a sport, not a livelihood. Jesus, though, was not inviting these men to occasional trips with him. He was calling them to the full-time work of discipleship, which involved inviting others to him.

DISCIPLES

Disciple means *one who learns from someone else and thus is a follower.* John the Baptist had disciples before Jesus called his group. Among Greek philosophers, Socrates had disciples who followed him, learned from him, and sometimes served him. In the Old Testament, Moses trained Joshua, and Elijah mentored Elisha.

Jesus had a large group of followers. From the crowds who followed him, Jesus selected a dozen, who were known as *The Twelve*. They went with him everywhere (see also Luke 8:2–3). They were free to ask him questions to understand his teachings more thoroughly. At some point Jesus trained them to do the work of ministry themselves. Apparently there were others who frequented his teaching and even the private sessions. In Acts 1:15–26 the gathered believers selected a replacement for Judas from two who were with them "from the beginning."

Today millions of people claim allegiance to Jesus. How good a disciple are you?

To their credit, all four simply left what they were doing and followed Jesus. James and John even left their father in the boat. Nothing was more important to them than Jesus' call. They asked no questions, required no promises.

Imagine another scenario. What if Jesus had described his exact plan to Peter at that point, including the road that ended in a cross? What if he had told Peter of the sacrifices Peter would be called on to make, concluding with his own death in Rome? We often wish we had all the answers as to what lies ahead. But would Peter still have followed? Would we? Maybe, but maybe not. So God allowed Peter to discover more as he grew and as situations developed. So Jesus reveals to us what we need to know as we need to know it. God's constant promise is always with us. Whatever comes, we will never face it alone!

The story is the model for all of us. Jesus still calls us to follow him, whatever the cost. The call to be a Christian is a radical call, demanding all we have. Indeed, with the presence and power of the Holy Spirit, we may give even more than we thought we could.

At one time, Baptists usually referred to the ministry as *full-time Christian service*. Now we understand that all Christians are called to *full-time service*. There are no part-time positions as Christians, whether you serve as pastor or work in a factory.

Jesus Proclaims and Heals (4:23–25)

Jesus began a tour of Galilee, northern Palestine, the area around his hometown of Nazareth and his current home of Capernaum. We have looked at the heart of Jesus' message ("repent," Matt. 4:17). As you study passages from the Sermon on the Mount in the next several lessons, you will get a synopsis of a typical day's teaching.

In addition to "teaching in their synagogues" and "preaching the good news of the kingdom," Jesus demonstrated his power by healing. He healed all kinds of diseases. He made the sick become well; he cast out demons; he relieved pain and reversed paralysis. Huge crowds came from everywhere to see and hear him. Many sick people came; others brought the sick to be healed. They came from surrounding territories, even Gentile country ("the Decapolis," or *Ten Cities*).

WAYS TO STRENGTHEN YOUR DISCIPLESHIP

- Recognize your sin, and repent deeply
- Study your Bible daily
- Pray regularly and systematically
- Share your faith with others
- Demonstrate Christlike compassion

Jesus created a sensation. The message went out, and people came. Those who heard told others, and those others came to see for themselves.

Implications and Applications

1. Biblical repentance requires change. Feeling sorry for your attitudes and behavior may be a start, but such sorrow is only a start. Real repentance reaches down to the motives that drive your behavior. Confessing those motives to yourself and to God (and perhaps to another trusted person) begins the road out. Changing those motives changes behavior. And changing behavior meets the Bible's requirement for repentance.

2. The New Testament is a book of hope. The kingdom of heaven is still breaking into our world. Christ is still active in the hearts and lives of his people. Many say that people never change. The Christian gospel says that is not true. When Christ breaks into one's life, one's life is forever changed.

3. Jesus made a difference in his world, and he calls us to change our world as well. He still selects disciples. We often discuss what's wrong with the world. Christ would impel us to do less talk and more action. Our mission is to proclaim the gospel in word and deed.

4. I've always been amazed by the simplicity and immediacy with which the first disciples followed Jesus. I keep looking back and

trying to hold onto various kinds of things I need to let go of. Do you? This Scripture passage compels us to follow with the same simple directness to see where Jesus will lead us.

QUESTIONS

1. When have you repented deeply of your sins? What issues does your conscience present to you today? What will you do about them?

2. Is your life positive and hopeful in the knowledge that you are part of God's kingdom? Do you share that confidence with others along with pointing out its source in Christ?

3. Do you consider yourself a disciple, a follower of Jesus? Do you follow Jesus' teachings and live by Jesus' standards? What keeps you from walking closer to Jesus?

4. When was the last time you shared the message of Christ with someone? Would you try to reach one more person for Christ this year than last?

Hope in Jesus' Teachings

One of the things that sets the Gospel of Matthew apart from the other Gospels is the amount of time Matthew devotes to Jesus' teachings. The Gospel of Matthew organizes Jesus' teachings into five major sections (Matthew 5—7; 10; 13; 18; 23—25). The Sermon on the Mount in Matthew 5—7 is the largest of the five sections. The lessons in this unit deal with Jesus' teachings in two of these sections, and the bonus lesson is from yet another section.

Lesson six ("The Great Reversal," Matt. 5:1–12) answers the question of what it means to live as a part of the kingdom of God. Jesus' expectations for his followers turn the world's values upside down. Lesson seven ("Praying Jesus' Way," 6:5–15) guides us to follow Jesus' example in prayer. Lesson eight ("Trust, Not Anxiety or Greed," 6:19–34) challenges us to trust and depend on God rather than being ruled by worry or greed. Lesson nine ("Realistic Encouragement," 13:1–23) encourages us with the knowledge that although some may reject Jesus' message, others will respond. Our responsibility is to share the truth; God produces the harvest.[1]

The common thread running through all these lessons has to do with Jesus' sure victory and certain reign. In his teachings, Jesus challenges us with what the attitudes and actions should be of those who belong to the kingdom of God. Those of us who call Jesus *Lord* are to live life under God's authority and rule. Jesus calls us to live differently from the way the unbelieving world lives.

Jesus inaugurated his kingdom during his earthly ministry, but it will not come fully on earth until the day Christ returns in glory. We live now with the tension of the in-between. Jesus' teachings show us how to live as we celebrate his resurrection and anticipate his return. We find hope in the certainty of Jesus' victory. Hard times will come, but we know the end of the story: Jesus wins.

UNIT THREE. HOPE IN JESUS' TEACHINGS

NOTES

1. Unless otherwise noted, all Scripture references and quotations in unit 3, lessons 6–9, are from the New American Standard Bible (1995 edition).

LESSON SIX
The Great Reversal

Most people would not call the year they were diagnosed with cancer *the best year of my life*. Melody does.

Melody was thirty-two years old when she was diagnosed with breast cancer, only two months after following God's leadership to move to another city. She describes her experience: "When I got the phone call, the first emotion was fear. And yet there was also the 'peace that passes understanding.' I had fear, but there was also peace. . . . I just had to trust that 'You are God.'"

When Melody first sent out an e-mail to friends about her diagnosis, she didn't ask them to pray for her healing. She asked them to pray that she would know God's love. That prayer has been answered

One of the greatest blessings God has brought Melody through this experience is her church community. Although she hadn't yet joined her church when she was diagnosed, the church embraced her.

"I have really experienced the love of Christ through the church," Melody says. "I wasn't sure how I was going to eat. They fed me. They went with me to the surgeon. They visited and gave me gift cards so I could buy clothes that fit. They paid for my mom to fly in for my surgery and treatments. They prayed for me like crazy. Most of all, there was this sense that they were glad to see me—that they really cared, that I wasn't a burden. Being able to walk into a huge church and see people that really loved me was just amazing."

God has also used Melody's cancer to teach her more about himself. "I have to say that God was drawing me closer to himself even before my diagnosis, and I think that would have continued, cancer or no cancer. Still, I have really learned to depend on him and him alone. There is a difference between 'You are all I have' and 'You are all I want.' That 'You are all I want' is the place I have come to through this."

God blesses his children. Those blessings don't always come in the shapes or forms we may expect. God's blessings do not ensure us an easy path; sometimes God's greatest blessings come in the face of the most trying circumstances. Still, God's blessings often have a way of blowing away all our expectations. Those divine blessings can make life in God's kingdom different from ordinary life.

MATTHEW 5:1–12

¹When Jesus saw the crowds, He went up on the mountain; and after He sat down, His disciples came to Him. ²He opened His mouth and began to teach them, saying, ³"Blessed are the poor in spirit, for theirs is the kingdom of heaven. ⁴"Blessed are those who mourn, for they shall be comforted. ⁵"Blessed are the gentle, for they shall inherit the earth. ⁶"Blessed are those who hunger and thirst for righteousness, for they shall be satisfied. ⁷"Blessed are the merciful, for they shall receive mercy. ⁸"Blessed are the pure in heart, for they shall see God. ⁹"Blessed are the peacemakers, for they shall be called sons of God. ¹⁰ "Blessed are those who have been persecuted for the sake of righteousness, for theirs is the kingdom of heaven. ¹¹"Blessed are you when people insult you and persecute you, and falsely say all kinds of evil against you because of Me. ¹²"Rejoice and be glad, for your reward in heaven is great; for in the same way they persecuted the prophets who were before you.

Setting and Context (5:1–2)

The Sermon on the Mount is the first of the five major sections on Jesus' teaching in the Gospel of Matthew. In the previous lesson, we saw that Jesus had called his first disciples and begun his public ministry. Large crowds were drawn to Jesus' teaching. Seeing the crowds, Jesus "went up on the mountain" and sat down to teach the disciples. Unlike today, when teachers usually stand in front of their classes, in Jesus' time Jewish teachers sat down to teach their followers. The fact that Jesus sat down before addressing his disciples (Matthew 5:1) helps show that he was an authoritative teacher.

Matthew tells us that Jesus' audience was his disciples. Although the crowds were listening in, Jesus was speaking to those who had already given him their allegiance and become citizens of the kingdom of God. In the Sermon on the Mount, Jesus told the disciples what kingdom life is really supposed to look like.

The World Turned Upside Down (5:3–12)

Jesus opened his sermon with the Beatitudes—eight short statements about those who are "blessed" or who experience the good life in the kingdom of God.[1] If we were asked to name characteristics of *the good life*, most of us would probably list things like good health, financial security, enjoyable work, and friends and family. Jesus gives us a much different list.

"Blessed are the poor in spirit." People who are "poor in spirit" acknowledge their need of and dependence on God. They demonstrate the opposite of the arrogance and pride the world seems to expect and to reward. Those who are poor in spirit acknowledge God's authority and gladly accept God's rule. Jesus said that "the poor in spirit" are blessed because "theirs is the kingdom of heaven." Those who recognize their dependence on God reap the benefits of God's rule in their lives.

"Blessed are those who mourn." One definition of the word translated "blessed" is *happy*. That definition seems incongruous. How can a person be happy and mourn at the same time? There are times in life when Christians mourn. Sometimes we weep over personal losses, but sometimes our hearts are broken when we see the fallen world around us. We mourn when we see how sin ravages people's lives, and we recognize once again that God's kingdom has not yet fully come, that Christ does not reign in the hearts of all people. The blessedness, or happiness, Jesus describes comes from the knowledge that those who mourn will one day be truly comforted. Jewish writers often used the passive voice such as "will be comforted" in order to avoid directly using the name of God. The meaning is that God will comfort those who mourn.

"Blessed are the gentle." Think for a moment about successful leaders in business and industry. What qualities are they known for? Most often it is for things such as passion, vision, drive, or charisma. Gentleness rarely makes the list. Citizens of God's kingdom are humble in their relationships with other people because they have first humbled themselves before God when they submitted to Christ as Lord. As believers, we do not need to *lord it over* people or exercise worldly power, for we know the One who is ultimately in control. Jesus says that the gentle will "inherit the earth." This indicates a reversal of fortune. James 4:10 says, "Humble yourselves before the Lord, and he will lift you up" (NIV). When we acknowledge God's sovereignty and surrender control to him, God rewards us beyond all expectation.

"Blessed are those who hunger and thirst for righteousness." The Apostle Paul is an example of one who hungered and thirsted after righteousness. Consider his words to the church in Philippi: "For to me, to live is Christ and to die is gain" (Philippians 1:21). Those who hunger and thirst after righteousness are those who eagerly desire to live in a manner pleasing to God and to see God's will done in and through them. They understand Jesus' rebuke to Satan during the temptation: "Man shall not live on bread alone, but on every word that proceeds out of the mouth of God" (Matt. 4:4). People who have this deep longing to please God will be "satisfied." In fact, they will not just be satisfied, but "satiated" or "stuffed!"[2] Again, the passive voice indicates that God alone will meet their deepest longings.

"Blessed are the merciful." To show mercy is to imitate the character of God. Being merciful is not just forgiving readily—although forgiveness is certainly part of it. showing mercy means demonstrating an attitude of compassion and grace toward others and patience with their failures. Mercy is shown in concrete acts toward others. God's children can be merciful because they have received mercy from God. Jesus promises that those who show mercy will be blessed because they will also receive mercy from our merciful Father.

"Blessed are the pure in heart." We tend to think of purity as the

TRUE BLESSING

The Greek word *makarios* translated "blessed" in Matthew 5:3–11 is a difficult one to grasp because there really is no good English equivalent. Some translations use *happy*, but we tend to use *happy* to describe an emotion rather than a state of being. *Happiness* also tends to be more fleeting, while *blessedness* describes something that is capable of enduring even in the midst of difficult circumstances. The New Testament concept is related to the Old Testament idea of the favorable condition of one who enjoys right relationship with God (see Psalm 1 for an example).

A helpful way of understanding "blessed" is to say that someone whom God has truly blessed is one with whom God is pleased or to whom God shows favor. Blessing is deeply rooted in a strong relationship with God. Those who are blessed can take comfort in the fact that no matter the difficulties they face, God is there.

absence of evil or contamination. In Scripture, however, being pure in heart describes those whose chief desire is to know God. Psalm 27:4 expresses it well: "One thing I have asked from the Lord, that I shall seek: That I may dwell in the house of the Lord all the days of my life, To behold the beauty of the Lord And to meditate in His temple." Those whose singlemost desire is an intimate relationship with God are blessed because "they shall see God." Their desire is realized in this life through a vibrant relationship with God and is ultimately fulfilled in eternity when they see God face to face.

"Blessed are the peacemakers." Kingdom citizens have a "ministry of reconciliation" given to them by God, who "was in Christ reconciling the world to Himself" (2 Corinthians 5:18–19). Peacemakers have more than just an amiable personality; peacemakers actively seek to reconcile people to one another and to God. During the time of Christ, the Roman Empire was largely at peace, ensured by the might of the Roman military. This lack of conflict did not ensure the presence of true peace, however. Only Christ could bring true peace in the sense of unbroken relationship, a relationship in which both parties seek the best interest of the other. Peacemakers, who are about God's work in the world, are recognized as belonging to God and "shall be called sons of God."

"Blessed are those who have been persecuted for the sake of righteousness." Darkness resists light, and those who stand for the kingdom will be opposed by those who are threatened by it. Jesus himself said, "I did not come to bring peace but a sword" (Matt. 10:34), recognizing the conflict that his disciples would face. This persecution is the result of righteous

CASE STUDY

Grace Baptist Church is located ten miles away from a state prison, which is one of the largest employers in the area. Quite frequently, mothers move into the local apartments to be close to their boyfriend or husband who is in jail. Many children in the school system have a parent who is in prison. Sometimes newly released prisoners stay in the area while they are on parole. What are some ways in which Grace Baptist can demonstrate the qualities of kingdom life described in Matthew 5:1–12 as they minister in this situation?

living. But the reward is great—heaven itself. In verses 11 and 12 Jesus elaborated on this point and made it personal: "Blessed are you."

When we exhibit the values of the kingdom—mercy rather than vengeance, humility rather than arrogance, purity rather than lust, mourning over evil rather than rejoicing in debauchery—the world takes notice. Some are inspired to seek the God who has made such a change in us, but some will do anything in their power to discredit us and our witness. In such times, we can take heart in the knowledge that we have an eternal home.

We can also take comfort in knowing that we are not the only ones who suffer. Throughout history, God's people have been persecuted for their stands. Yet we also know that God and his people ultimately triumph.

Implications and Actions

It is important to realize that the Beatitudes and the Sermon on the Mount are to be taken descriptively rather than prescriptively. That is, Jesus was describing qualities that should be present in the life of the believer, not laying out a list of entrance requirements for heaven.[3] These qualities are the distinctive characteristics of the new covenant. In the Sermon on the Mount, Jesus does not so much proclaim a new law as fulfill an old promise—a law that is written on our hearts (Jeremiah 31:33). We achieve these things not by human effort but by the transforming work of the Spirit, who continually shapes us into the image of Christ. The marks of a believer Jesus lays out in Matthew 5:3–16 are made possible only by the indwelling power of the Holy Spirit.

There should be something unmistakably different about a Christian's life. Those who have truly made Christ Lord of their lives have a different set of priorities than the world does. Rather than worshiping self, we strive to bring glory to God. That difference must be demonstrated in our lives both in words and in action. Can those around you see your light shine?

QUESTIONS

1. How do you see the qualities Jesus listed in Matthew 5:1–12 demonstrated in your church community?

2. In what ways do the Beatitudes reverse the world's expectations?

3. What differences do you think someone who does not know Christ might see in your life because of your relationship with God?

4. Have you ever experienced—or do you know someone who has experienced—persecution because of a stand the person took for the gospel? What gave you (or the person) hope through that situation?

5. Which of the blessings described in the Beatitudes have you experienced personally?

NOTES

1. Although some people count verse 11 as a ninth beatitude, because of its length and the shift from "those" to "you" I consider it a bridge statement between the beatitudes and the following illustration of salt and light in Matt. 5:13–16.

2. R.T. France, *The Gospel of Matthew*, New International Commentary on the New Testament (William B. Eerdmans Publishing, Grand Rapids: Michigan, 2007), 168.

3. Douglas R. A. Hare, *Matthew*. Interpretation, A Bible Commentary for Teaching and Preaching (Louisville, John Knox, 1993), 35.

FOCAL TEXT
Matthew 6:5–15

BACKGROUND
Matthew 6:1–18

MAIN IDEA
Followers of Jesus are to pray as Jesus instructed, thus acknowledging their utter dependence on God for all aspects of their lives.

QUESTION TO EXPLORE
How does Jesus' instruction about prayer differ from popular ideas about prayer?

STUDY AIM
To decide to change how I approach prayer in accord with Jesus' instructions

QUICK READ
Praying as Jesus prayed means acknowledging our dependence on God as we pray for both our own needs and the work of God's kingdom. God is our only audience in prayer.

LESSON SEVEN
Praying Jesus' Way

73

What I remember as my first personal encounter with prayer came when I was an older pre-teen. My family was facing a move, and I was sure my world was about to end. One night at a youth lock-in at church, my best friend and I slipped away from the group and found a quiet place to pray. We knelt down and asked God to let me stay. What I remember most from that moment is a sudden certainty that God was listening and that he cared.

Over the next few weeks God continued to draw me to seek him. As I prayed and read my Bible, I finally came to a place where I was able to say: "Okay, God—you know what I want. But I'm willing to do and to be whatever you want. Doing your will is what I want most." Through prayer, God brought me to a point of surrender.

As it turned out, my family didn't move. As a pre-teen, I rejoiced that God had answered my prayers. Looking back now, I realize that even if we had moved, God still had answered me. God used that experience in my life to teach me something about prayer as an expression of my relationship to God and to bring me to a new level of dependence on him. Through my first crisis of faith, I began to learn to find hope in God rather than in my circumstances and to understand prayer as more than a wish list. Although I am still learning those lessons as an adult, I look back on that time as the beginning point of my faith journey. It was a time when I began consciously attempting to follow Jesus' example for prayer.

MATTHEW 6:5–15

⁵"When you pray, you are not to be like the hypocrites; for they love to stand and pray in the synagogues and on the street corners so that they may be seen by men. Truly I say to you, they have their reward in full. ⁶"But you, when you pray, go into your inner room, close your door and pray to your Father who is in secret, and your Father who sees what is done in secret will reward you. ⁷"And when you are praying, do not use meaningless repetition as the Gentiles do, for they suppose that they will be heard for their many words. ⁸"So do not be like them; for your Father knows what you need before you ask Him. ⁹"Pray, then, in this way: 'Our Father who is in heaven, Hallowed be Your name. ¹⁰'Your kingdom

come. Your will be done, On earth as it is in heaven. ¹¹'Give us this day our daily bread. ¹²'And forgive us our debts, as we also have forgiven our debtors. ¹³'And do not lead us into temptation, but deliver us from evil. [For Yours is the kingdom and the power and the glory forever. Amen].' ¹⁴"For if you forgive others for their transgressions, your heavenly Father will also forgive you. ¹⁵"But if you do not forgive others, then your Father will not forgive your transgressions.

Be Perfect

In Matthew 5:17–20, Jesus began his explanation of his relationship to the Old Testament law. Jesus came not to abolish the law, but to fulfill it (Matthew 5:17). Through our relationship with Christ, believers keep the law as an expression of our love for God that overflows into our treatment of other people. In Matthew 5:21–48, Jesus used six examples to illustrate this truth. Not only are we to refrain from murder, but we are also to pursue peace in all relationships; not only are we prohibited from adultery but we are also to maintain purity of heart and mind. In the areas of divorce, keeping our word, retaliation, and treatment of our enemies, Jesus calls Christians to keep the spirit of the law, not only the letter of it. Our response is made possible by the power of the Spirit. Jesus summed it up in Matthew 5:48: "Therefore, you are to be perfect, as your heavenly Father is perfect."

Proper Practice

As just mentioned, in Matthew 5:17–48 Jesus gave a general principle about the law and then illustrated it with six examples. Jesus did something similar in the following chapter. In Matthew 6:1, Jesus warned us that God alone is to be the audience of all our worship and religious practice. He illustrated his point through teaching his followers about the proper motivation for giving, praying, and fasting.

Jesus' teachings assumed that his followers would pray, give, and fast. His concern is that we engage in such practices with the proper attitude.

Giving to the poor should not be done to make others think well of us, but rather as a quiet act of service to God (Matt. 6:2–4.). Similarly, we do not fast so others will applaud our piousness, but as a sign of humility and dependence on God (6:16–18).

Audience and Attitude

Jesus used two contrasts to show us what our audience and attitude should be like in prayer. First, Jesus described the "hypocrites," who prayed ostentatiously in public places "so that they may be seen by men" (6:6).

This attitude is not for followers of Christ; our only audience in prayer is God. In prayer, we expose our hearts before God. Prayer is not the time to teach a lesson, impress others with flowery phrases, or get in a little *dig* at someone else's expense. This is not to say that prayer should always be private. Jesus prayed publicly as well as privately, and the model prayer Jesus gave us in Matthew 6:9–13 has a corporate nature. The question is one of audience. When we pray to be noticed by those around us, we get what we want—and that is our only reward. When we pray as a genuine expression of our relationship to God, God hears and rewards us.

Jesus also used the example of the Gentiles to show the attitude with which we should pray. In Jesus' time, Gentiles, or non-Jewish people,

---

HYPOCRITE

The word "hypocrite" was originally used for actors in a Greek play who used different masks in order to play different roles. Jesus often used the term to condemn the actions of the Pharisees, who used outward religious actions to mask their inner corruption. They were like "whitewashed tombs" (Matt. 23:27), which looked good on the outside but were filled with death and decay inside.

Jesus rebuked the Pharisees for actions such as giving in order to impress others (6:2) and tithing spices while neglecting more important matters such as justice and mercy (23:23). Their actions were like those who meticulously cleaned the outside of a cup while ignoring the dirt inside it (23:25). Today we use the term to describe a person who says one thing but does the opposite of what he or she says.

often prayed loudly with much repetition of meaningless phrases. Pagan worshipers regarded prayer as a kind of magic formula. If they prayed in the right way with the right words, repeated themselves enough to make sure the gods understood them correctly, and proved themselves worthy of receiving an answer, then the gods would have to respond. This is not the attitude Christians should have in prayer.

Prayer is a means of communication, not a way to manipulate God into giving us what we want. We don't need to impress God with our religious vocabulary, and neither do we have to win God's favor by making outrageous promises: "God, if you'll only _____, I promise I'll never _____ again!" We pray not to some unconcerned or absent deity but to our loving Father who "knows what you need before you ask Him" (6:8). God knows, cares, and wants to answer our prayers.

Praying for His Glory

In Matthew 6:9–13, Jesus gave his disciples a pattern to follow in prayer. In Jesus' time, rabbis often gave their followers model prayers, in which each line reminded their followers of certain topics about which they were to pray. In the same way, Jesus' prayer serves as a model for our prayer. The prayer is composed of two basic parts: worship and petition.

"Our Father who is in heaven." Jesus often referred to God as Father. In the Lord's Prayer, Jesus calls God "Our Father." Through Christ, we are adopted into the family of God and have the privilege of calling on God as our loving Father. Prayer is an expression of an intimate relationship with God. Yet in prayer we also acknowledge God's holiness and sovereignty. When we recognize that God's dwelling place is in heaven, we acknowledge God's perfection and submit ourselves to God's power and authority.

"Hallowed be Your name." "Hallowed," or *holy*, means *set apart*. When we recognize that God's name is holy, we recognize that God is holy. It is a recognition of God's absolute perfection in all things. When we pray, "Hallowed be Your name," we worship God in his holiness and perfection, but we also pray that God will demonstrate his power and holiness so that all people will recognize the greatness of his name.

"Your kingdom come." The kingdom of God has both a *now* and a *not yet* quality. In one sense, the kingdom of God is present now wherever

people submit themselves to God's authority and ultimate rule. Still, there is another sense, the *not yet* view of the kingdom, in which we anticipate the day of Christ's return when he will establish his kingdom fully. When we pray "your kingdom come," we anticipate Christ's second coming and look forward to that day when "every knee will bow and every tongue confess that Jesus Christ is Lord" (Philippians 2:11). Yet we are also concerned with the here and now. When we pray "your kingdom come," we are praying that God's rule will be more firmly established in our lives, church, community, and world. We pray for those who have never heard the name of Christ to embrace his rule and become citizens of the kingdom. We pray for God's sovereignty to be demonstrated through the work and ministry of our church, and we commit ourselves to action.

"Your will be done On earth as it is in heaven." In heaven God's will is done perfectly. On earth sin and evil prevent God's will from being done in our lives and in the world around us. When we pray "your will be done," we commit ourselves to doing God's will.

Many times as Christians we get so wrapped up in such matters as what job we should take or what college we should go to that we forget that large portions of God's will for us are already revealed in Scripture. We must commit to do what God has already revealed to us as well as submit to the specifics God will show us in the future. For God to accomplish his will in our churches and communities, we have to be willing to be a part of God's work.

Praying with Petitions

The last three clauses of the Lord's Prayer have to do with our own needs. The corporate nature of the prayer is also demonstrated here. We are concerned not only for our own personal needs, but also for the needs of those around us.

"Give us this day our daily bread." In Jesus' time bread was a major staple of the diet in Israel. Day laborers were paid each day for their work, thus enabling them to buy food for their families for that day. Missing a few days of work because of illness or injury could be devastating.

Praying for our daily bread echoes the experience of Israel during the Exodus. God provided manna daily for the people—but only enough for that day. The manna came fresh every morning, reminding the people of their constant dependence on God (Exodus 16:14–32). In our Western culture with monthly paychecks, deep freezers, and warehouse stores, we may feel removed from this idea of daily dependency. God still desires to meet our needs. We are challenged to recognize that God is our provider and that all we need ultimately comes to us from God's hand.

"And forgive us our debts, as we also have forgiven our debtors." Jesus further explained this point in verses 14–15. If we forgive others, God will forgive us, but if we do not forgive others, God will not forgive us. It is not so much that we earn forgiveness by forgiving, but that our attitudes toward others demonstrate we have been forgiven. We should not expect to receive from God what we are not willing to give to others.

Sometimes people have a false understanding of forgiveness. Forgiveness does not mean being a doormat for others' mistreatment. Forgiveness means relinquishing the right to our own vengeance and leaving justice with God. Forgiveness is a refusal to hold others' sins against them and coming to that place where we desire God's will for them—whatever that may be. When we, as God's people, experience God's forgiveness, God empowers us through his Spirit to extend forgiveness to others.

"And do not lead us into temptation, but deliver us from evil." God cannot be tempted, and neither does God tempt anyone (James 1:13–14). When we pray "do not lead us into temptation," we acknowledge our own weakness and pray that God will give us the strength to resist

HOW TO APPLY THIS LESSON

- As you pray, pay attention to the different words and phrases that you use as you pray. Do you really mean all of them or know what they all mean? (For example, what does praying "in Jesus' name" really mean?) Try to discern what you pray with meaning, and what you are reciting out of habit.

- Use the Lord's Prayer as a pattern for your prayer life this week.

- As a class or small group, select an unreached people group to pray for on a regular basis. You can find information on people groups on websites such as www.peoplegroups.org.

temptation. Some think that "evil" here is an allusion to the evil one, or Satan, who seeks to "steal and kill and destroy" (John 10:10). But we know that Satan is already defeated by the power of the cross. We can pray with confidence, knowing that "no temptation has seized you except what is common to man. And God is faithful: he will not let you be tempted beyond what you can bear. But when you are tempted he will also provide you a way out so that you can stand up under it" (1 Corinthians 10:13, NIV). When we depend on God, God gives us the ability to be obedient to him.

Implications and Actions

Jesus' teachings about prayer show us how we should approach prayer. We pray not to gain people's approval, but God's. We pray to our loving and caring Father with an attitude of faith and trust rather than manipulation and attention seeking. In prayer, we are concerned not only for our own needs, but also for the needs of others and for the work of the kingdom of God in our world.

Jesus' model prayer gives us hope, for we know that God is at work in our world and hears our prayers. It also reminds us to look forward to that day when the kingdom will fully come and Christ's victory will be fully established on earth. His victory is what we both anticipate and celebrate in prayer.

QUESTIONS

1. What are some popular misconceptions people have about prayer? How do those ideas affect the way people pray?

2. In times of corporate prayer, how do you keep your attention focused on God rather than on others?

3. What does it mean for you to pray the way Jesus prayed?

4. How are the different components of the Lord's Prayer reflected in your prayer life? in the prayers of your church?

5. How do we keep a balance between praying for the needs of the kingdom and praying for our own needs? Which comes more naturally for us?

FOCAL TEXT
Matthew 6:19–34

BACKGROUND
Matthew 6:19—7:29

MAIN IDEA
Jesus calls us to trust God and focus our lives on God's way rather than on material things.

QUESTION TO EXPLORE
Do we really value God more than we value things?

STUDY AIM
To consider how my life would be changed if I trusted God and focused my life more on God's way rather than on material things

QUICK READ
Trusting God and focusing on God's way rather than on material things frees us from anxiety and worry as we learn to depend on God to meet our needs.

LESSON EIGHT
Trust, Not Anxiety or Greed

83

I have to admit worry comes naturally to me. After all, we live in uncertain times. As I write this, recent news included mass shootings at a shopping mall, a church, and a university. We fear terrorist attacks, global warming, bird flu, a Social Security meltdown, lack of health care—and more.

Some worries we bring on ourselves directly. According to one estimate, the average American family has $8,000 in credit card debt, and almost half of all families spend more than they make in a year.[1] We have more things to spend money on and more ways to spend it than ever before. Our greed traps us in a cycle of worry and fear.

This is not what God wants for his children! God does not want us to be slaves to worry or to be trapped by our selfish desires. The life Jesus described in the Sermon on the Mount is a life characterized by trust and dependence rather than anxiety and greed. To live lives free from anxiety and greed, we must discover what is truly important. We must focus our lives on God's way, rather than on gaining material things. As we trust God and focus on God's way, God calls us to change our treasure, our outlook on life, and the kingdom we seek.

MATTHEW 6:19–34

[19]"Do not store up for yourselves treasures on earth, where moth and rust destroy, and where thieves break in and steal. [20]"But store up for yourselves treasures in heaven, where neither moth nor rust destroys, and where thieves do not break in or steal; [21]for where your treasure is, there your heart will be also. [22]"The eye is the lamp of the body; so then if your eye is clear, your whole body will be full of light. [23]"But if your eye is bad, your whole body will be full of darkness. If then the light that is in you is darkness, how great is the darkness! [24]"No one can serve two masters; for either he will hate the one and love the other, or he will be devoted to one and despise the other. You cannot serve God and wealth. [25]"For this reason I say to you, do not be worried about your life, as to what you will eat or what you will drink; nor for your body, as to what you will put on. Is not life more than food, and the body more than clothing? [26]"Look at the birds of the air, that they do not sow, nor reap nor gather into barns, and yet your heavenly Father

feeds them. Are you not worth much more than they? [27]"And who of you by being worried can add a single hour to his life? [28]"And why are you worried about clothing? Observe how the lilies of the field grow; they do not toil nor do they spin, [29]yet I say to you that not even Solomon in all his glory clothed himself like one of these. [30]"But if God so clothes the grass of the field, which is alive today and tomorrow is thrown into the furnace, will He not much more clothe you? You of little faith! [31]"Do not worry then, saying, 'What will we eat?' or 'What will we drink?' or 'What will we wear for clothing?' [32]"For the Gentiles eagerly seek all these things; for your heavenly Father knows that you need all these things. [33]"But seek first His kingdom and His righteousness, and all these things will be added to you. [34]"So do not worry about tomorrow; for tomorrow will care for itself. Each day has enough trouble of its own.

Storing the Right Treasure (6:19–21)

When our focus is on God and God's way, what is most precious to us changes. Rather than trying to gain material things, we desire the blessings that come from pleasing God. Storing the right treasure frees us from worry and greed because heavenly treasures cannot be destroyed.

Instead of material possessions, which are easily lost or destroyed, Jesus urges us to "store up treasures in heaven" (Matt 6:20). In New Testament times people stored their wealth in their homes. Gold, jewelry, and valuable textiles were all vulnerable to decay or theft. We may not fear moth and rust today, but our wealth is vulnerable to threats such as natural disaster, identity theft, and catastrophic illness. Thankfully, heavenly treasure does not decay and cannot be stolen. These heavenly treasures are not part of a tit-for-tat system in which good deeds are exchanged for heavenly riches. Rather they are the rewards of living in obedience to God. Heavenly riches are the blessings we receive when we live according to God's priorities.

Someone once asked me, "Could other people tell you're a Christian by looking at your checkbook?" The things we invest our money and time in reveal our priorities. Following God's way frees us from worry and fear because we know God's kingdom will not pass away. When we are consumed with worry and fear over losing *stuff*, our anxiety reveals that God is not first in our hearts. "Where your treasure is, there your heart will be also" (6:21).

Having the Right Outlook (6:22–24)

When we focus on God and God's way, God also changes how we view our possessions. We begin seeing our money and time as gifts to be used, not things to be hoarded. Jesus used an illustration of the *good eye* to teach his followers how they should view their possessions.

On a mission trip to Central Asia a few years ago, I noticed that many homes and cars had unusual decorations in their windows. I learned

---

JESUS ON MONEY

It is interesting to note the number of times Jesus taught about money and wealth in the Gospels. Many of Jesus' parables use money as a symbol of how we invest our lives or as an indicator of our relationship with God. Jesus also spoke directly about money and how it affects our spiritual life. Here is a brief summary of some of Jesus' teachings:

- Wealth can be a distraction from hearing the gospel and an obstacle to serving God whole-heartedly (Matt. 19:16–26).

- A small gift given with sincere sacrifice is more precious to God than a large amount that costs the giver little (Mark 12:41–44).

- Wealth is meant to be used rather than hoarded. It is foolish to store up wealth but give no thought to eternity (Luke 12:16–21).

- Wealth can be a blessing when used in service to God. Jesus' public ministry was supported by generous gifts from wealthy women such as Joanna and Susanna (Luke 8:1–3).

- When we serve the Lord, we should trust in him to provide for us rather than trusting in our own resources (Mark 6:8)

that these decorations were protections against the *evil eye*. The people believed that if another person was envious of something one had, one could put the *evil eye* on that item so that the envious person would lose it or it would become useless to him or her.

The idea of the *good* or "clear" eye and the "bad eye" (6:22–23) is similar. In the Old Testament, a generous person was said to have a "good eye," while a selfish or greedy person had an *evil* or "bad" eye (see Proverbs 28:22). A person who is generous and willing to share with others views life differently from one who is selfish and greedy.

It's easy to find excuses not to give. *Those people need to go out and get jobs*, or *If I give him something he's just going to drink it away*. Perhaps we worry about being cheated or feel that we should see to our own needs before giving. We need to use wisdom and discretion in our giving, but we also need to examine our hearts. Sometimes our reasons for holding back are really excuses to avoid sacrifice. Viewing life with generosity and grace frees us from worry and greed.

Jesus said, "No one can serve two masters" (Matt. 6:24). Here, Jesus was referring to slavery. Unlike today, when many people work two jobs, slaves were completely owned by their masters. It was a total commitment. If we try to be committed both to God and to wealth, we will always choose one at the cost of the other. Our lives reveal what is the most important to us.

When faced with keeping your job or maintaining your integrity, what do you choose? How do you advise your teen when his or her manager requires your teen to work the Sunday morning shift? How do you respond when God places a need on your heart? What if filling this need requires giving up what you had set aside for your vacation or a new electronic gadget?

If God is first in our lives, we will willingly make sacrifices when God requires it of us. If our own desires are first, we will compromise when obedience to God conflicts with our financial security. We cannot serve two masters.

Seeking the Right Kingdom (6:25–34)

When we focus on God and God's way, God leads us to seek his kingdom rather than our own. We learn to desire God's pleasure more than our own way. As we surrender our wants and trust God to meet our needs, God frees us from anxiety and greed.

Jesus' first major point in this passage is that his followers should not be anxious over basic needs such as food or clothing. Our life should be about more than the pursuit of possessions. "Is not life more than food, and the body more than clothing?" (6:25).

Even those who reach the top of their fields often find that something is still missing. Tom Brady, quarterback for the New England Patriots, said in a 2007 interview: "Why do I have three Superbowl rings and still think there's something greater out there for me? I mean, maybe a lot of people would say, 'Hey man, this is what it is.' I reached my goal, my dream, my life. Me, I think . . . it's got to be more than this."[2] There is something within us that wealth and fame will never satisfy. That *something more* we all need is found in following God and God's way.

Jesus used the example of the birds to remind us not to worry about food. Birds don't plant or harvest, but God meets their needs. The birds are a reminder to trust in God's provision. If God sees to the needs of the sparrows, will God not see to mine? "Are you not worth much more than they?" (6:26) If God is truly our master, we can trust God to take care of our needs.

Jesus also said not to worry because worry accomplishes nothing. "Who of you by being worried can add a single hour to his life?" (6:27). Worry produces inaction because fear paralyzes us. Worry does nothing, but prayer does everything. "Be anxious for nothing, but in everything by prayer and supplication with thanksgiving let your requests be known to God. And the peace of God, which surpasses all understanding will guard your hearts and your minds in Christ Jesus" (Philippians 4:6–7).

Jesus used the example of the flowers to exhort us not to worry about clothes (Matt 6:28–30). Each spring I am amazed at the beauty of the South Texas wildflowers. God extravagantly clothes the flowers, and yet they live for only a short time before they are scorched in the summer sun. How much more will God provide for us?

Jesus' second major point is that we should not worry because God already knows our needs (6:31–32). Worry reveals our lack of faith because it shows we are depending on ourselves rather than on God. Unlike those who do not know God, we serve a loving Father who knows our needs before we even ask (6:8). Because God already knows our needs, we can trust God to take care of us.

CASE STUDY

A young couple in your church comes to you for advice. God has been dealing with them in the area of finances, and they feel led to begin tithing. However, they have recently bought their first home, are both paying back student loans, are making payments on two new cars, and have $6,000 in credit card debt. They also want to start a family.

They want to be obedient to God, and yet they can't see how to make ends meet if they give ten percent of their income. What do you advise them to do?

Jesus' third major point is the key to avoiding worry and greed: "Seek first his kingdom and his righteousness, and all these things will be added to you" (6:33). *Seeking God's kingdom first* means that doing God's will is our first priority. We thus are more concerned with God's honor than our own. We allow God to reign over every area of our lives: our finances, families, and jobs. Every day in both big and small decisions, we choose to submit our attitude and actions to God. As we do, God gives us the strength to be obedient to him.

Through this process of daily submission, God refines our character and transforms our desires so that we hunger first after God and his way. It has been said that only three things are eternal: God; God's word; and the souls of people. As we learn to seek God's kingdom, the focus of our lives becomes these things. In every aspect of our lives we seek to worship God, to obey God's word, and to lead those around us to seek God. Our increasing trust and dependence on God frees us from anxiety and fear.

Finally, Jesus urges us not to borrow trouble. "Do not worry about tomorrow, for tomorrow will care for itself. Each day has enough trouble of its own" (6:34). This does not mean that we do not plan for the future. There is a place for emergency funds, college savings accounts, and retirement plans. The distinction is that we depend on God to meet our needs rather than depending on ourselves. All that we have comes from God. As God meets our needs for today, we can be assured that God will also provide for us tomorrow, no matter what comes.

The Sum of the Matter (7:1–29)

Jesus ended the Sermon on the Mount with additional encouragement for righteous living. We are not to come to these teachings like children pointing fingers. Before we judge others, we must first apply God's word to our own hearts and lives. Jesus reminds us of God's heart for his children. As a good father gives his children things that are good and not harmful, God gives us what is best. We do not have to fear that God is out to get us or worry that God will be stingy with his blessings. We can confidently pray to our loving Father, who joyfully meets his children's needs. We know also that our lives testify to what is important to us. The fruit of our lives reveals which master we serve.

Jesus told a brief parable of two foundations. The foolish man builds his house on the sand, which is washed away by the storm. The wise man builds his house on the rock, and the foundation stands firm. We must choose what we build our lives on. If we build our lives on fulfilling our own desires, they will eventually come crashing down around us. If we build on the foundation of God's ways and obedience to God's word, we know that we have a foundation that is secure. When storms come—and they will come—we can know that God is there and that he will keep us safe through them. Building our lives on the foundation of God's word frees us from worry and greed.

Final Thoughts

Trusting God and focusing our lives on God's will frees us from anxiety and greed. We can rest in God's promises to meet our needs when we do God's will.

Does this mean that things will never get tough? Of course not. Consider the Apostle Paul, who passionately loved the Lord and sought his kingdom. Yet even Paul endured suffering: "I have learned how to be content in whatever circumstances I am. I know how to get along with humble means, and I also know how to live in prosperity; in any and every circumstance I have learned the secret of being filled and going hungry, both of having abundance and suffering need. I can do all things through Him who strengthens me" (Phil. 4:11–13).

When we build up heavenly treasures, view life with generosity and grace, and seek God's kingdom first, God transforms something within us. He produces in us a contentment and a peace that transcends our circumstances and gives us a hope that will not disappoint. That is something to truly celebrate.

QUESTIONS

1. Using a concordance (perhaps at the back of your Bible), do a quick survey of what the New Testament teaches about money and giving. What conclusions can you draw from your study?

2. Consider the top five demands on your money, energy, and time. Which of these things honor God? Why or why not?

3. Is there anything you own you would not be willing to sacrifice if God asked it of you?

4. What things or situations in your life tempt you the most to worry? How can you begin to depend on God in those situations?

5. Who do you know who seeks God first in all things? How would you describe them? How have you seen them respond to difficult situations?

NOTES

1. Kim Khan, "How Does Your Debt Compare," MSN Money, www.moneycentral.msn.com/content/SavingandDebt/P70581.asp, accessed 7/10/08.

2. "Tom Brady, the Winner," CBS News 60 Minutes, December 23, 2007, www.cbsnews.com/stories/205/11/03/60minutes/printable1008148.shtml, accessed 7/10/08.

MAIN IDEA

Even though all will not respond to Jesus' message, the reality that many will respond means we must continue to share it.

QUESTION TO EXPLORE

What's the point of sharing Jesus' message when so many don't respond?

STUDY AIM

To identify what the parable of the sower and the soils means for my life, my church, and the mission of Jesus

QUICK READ

When we share the message of Christ, we can confidently hope in the knowledge that although some reject the gospel, some will respond. God brings forth the harvest.

LESSON NINE
Realistic Encouragement

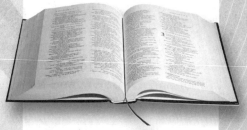

"My wife wants you to tell her how to become a Christian."

My husband and I met Yoshi and his wife through the English classes and Bible studies that we offered in our work with international students in Seattle, where we began our ministry. I knew that she had become increasingly interested in the gospel, but Yoshi's request on behalf of his wife was still a surprise. I gladly met with his wife and was pleased to learn that she had prayed to receive Christ and was planning to be baptized.

Working with international students had many rewarding aspects. We had opportunities to meet the best and the brightest from all over the world. Students who were leaders in the fields of medicine, government, business, and technology all came to the University of Washington to study. Many were from countries with limited access to the gospel. We had the joy of seeing a Chinese businessman realize for the first time that Christmas was a Christian holiday. A Vietnamese doctor told us that she wanted to return home and tell her friends what she had learned about Jesus. A South Korean student moved from being hostile to the gospel to desiring to use his business contacts as inroads for sharing Christ in North Korea.

Our ministry was discouraging at times, though. We treasured the relationships we were able to build with our international friends, but for every one who responded to the gospel, many did not. Some simply did not believe in God. For others, the message of Christ didn't make sense. Others were interested, but the pressures of school, finances, and family kept them from seeking more. There were days when we wondered why we bothered.

But we always had hope. We knew we were planting seeds and prayed that God would bring the increase. We believed that even if we didn't see the harvest, God would still bring it to pass. Although many did not respond, some always did. That hope kept us going.

MATTHEW 13:1–23

¹That day Jesus went out of the house and was sitting by the sea. ²And large crowds gathered to Him, so He got into a boat and sat down, and the whole crowd was standing on the beach. ³And He spoke many things to them in parables, saying,

"Behold, the sower went out to sow; ⁴and as he sowed, some [seeds] fell beside the road, and the birds came and ate them up. ⁵"Others fell on the rocky places, where they did not have much soil; and immediately they sprang up, because they had no depth of soil. ⁶"But when the sun had risen, they were scorched; and because they had no root, they withered away. ⁷"Others fell among the thorns, and the thorns came up and choked them out. ⁸"And others fell on the good soil and yielded a crop, some a hundredfold, some sixty, and some thirty. ⁹"He who has ears, let him hear."

¹⁰And the disciples came and said to Him, "Why do You speak to them in parables?" ¹¹Jesus answered them, "To you it has been granted to know the mysteries of the kingdom of heaven, but to them it has not been granted. ¹²"For whoever has, to him [more] shall be given, and he will have an abundance; but whoever does not have, even what he has shall be taken away from him. ¹³"Therefore I speak to them in parables; because while seeing they do not see, and while hearing they do not hear, nor do they understand. ¹⁴"In their case the prophecy of Isaiah is being fulfilled, which says, 'You will keep on hearing, but will not understand; You will keep on seeing, but will not perceive; ¹⁵For the heart of this people has become dull, With their ears they scarcely hear, And they have closed their eyes, Otherwise they would see with their eyes, Hear with their ears, And understand with their heart and return, And I would heal them.' ¹⁶"But blessed are your eyes, because they see; and your ears, because they hear. ¹⁷"For truly I say to you that many prophets and righteous men desired to see what you see, and did not see [it], and to hear what you hear, and did not hear [it].

¹⁸"Hear then the parable of the sower. ¹⁹"When anyone hears the word of the kingdom and does not understand it, the evil [one] comes and snatches away what has been sown in his heart. This is the one on whom seed was sown beside the road. ²⁰"The one on whom seed was sown on the rocky places, this is the man who hears the word and immediately receives it with joy; ²¹yet he has no [firm] root in himself, but is [only] temporary, and when affliction or persecution arises because of the word, immediately he falls

away. 22 And the one on whom seed was sown among the thorns, this is the man who hears the word, and the worry of the world and the deceitfulness of wealth choke the word, and it becomes unfruitful. 23 "And the one on whom seed was sown on the good soil, this is the man who hears the word and understands it; who indeed bears fruit and brings forth, some a hundredfold, some sixty, and some thirty."

Ministry in the Face of Growing Opposition (13:1–3)

Matthew 13 is the third of five major sections of Jesus' teachings in the Gospel of Matthew. In Matthew 8—12, Jesus continued to draw crowds but also faced increasing persecution. As Jesus performed public miracles such as the healing of the centurion's servant (Matthew 8:5–13) and the raising of Jairus's daughter (Matt. 9:18–30), the crowds following Jesus grew. Opposition from the Pharisees also increased. Jesus responded by commissioning the twelve disciples and sending them out to minister. He also directly confronted the Pharisees in his teaching, revealing their hypocrisy. Because of this, the Pharisees began plotting ways to destroy Jesus.

In Matthew 13, Jesus addressed the crowds. As Jesus was sitting by the sea, the crowds came to him. Jesus and his disciples climbed into a boat, and he addressed the crowds. Matthew 13:3 says that Jesus taught them "many things in parables."

This is the first use of the word "parable" in the Gospel of Matthew. We get the word "parable" from the Greek translation of a Hebrew word meaning *wise saying*. The parables of Jesus mostly take the form of a story with a hidden meaning. One of the important characteristics of a parable is that a parable takes thought and reflection in order to discover the hidden truth. While some people try to interpret the parables allegorically so that every element of the parable corresponds to some spiritual truth, most scholars identify each parable as teaching one major truth, or at least a limited number of major truths. Too, what the parables meant then forms the basis for their meaning for us today.

WILLIAM CAREY: "EXPECT GREAT THINGS ... ATTEMPT GREAT THINGS"

William Carey (1761–1834) is known today as the father of the modern mission movement. As a cobbler and pastor of a small church in England, Carey became convinced that the church had an obligation to preach the gospel to people who had never heard. Although he faced opposition, his work eventually led to the formation of the Particular Baptist Missionary Society. Carey was commissioned as one of the first missionaries, and he and his family left for India in 1793.

The early years in India were difficult. Following the death of their son, Carey's wife grew increasingly depressed. He labored in India for seven years with little support before baptizing his first Hindu convert in 1800. Although the early years of his ministry had little visible result, his forty years of service in India laid the groundwork not only for missions in India, but for the missions movement as we know it today.[2]

The Parable Told (13:3–9)

This first parable of Jesus in Matthew's Gospel is a key to the others in that it explains the different ways in which the crowds responded to Jesus' teaching. Jesus used an image that would have been very familiar to his audience: a farmer sowing seed. Some scholars think the parable reflects the common practice of broadcast sowing in which seed was cast broadly by hand and some inevitably fell on poor ground. Others think the parable may describe a farming technique in which seed was first cast and then tilled into the ground. Regardless, the emphasis is on the four types of soil and the plants produced.

In the first case, seeds fell on the path and were eaten by the birds before they had time to take root. Other seeds fell on rocky ground and quickly sprouted. These seeds could not withstand the sun's heat and withered because of having shallow roots. For the third group, the problem was not that of resources but of competition. The seeds fell on ground taken up by weeds, and the thorny weeds choked the plants' growth. Finally—and most importantly—some seeds fell on good soil and produced a bountiful crop. Scholars disagree on whether the amount of fruit produced was an exceptional crop or merely a good one, but the point is this: some seeds would inevitably bear fruit.

Why Parables? (13:10–17)

After Jesus told the parable, his disciples came to him with a question. This conversation could have occurred while they were still in the boat out of earshot of the crowd or at a later time. Either way, it is important to recognize that Jesus' teachings in this passage were addressed to his inner circle of followers, not to the crowd at large.

The disciples asked Jesus, "Why do You speak to them in parables?" (Matt 13:10). Jesus' response has something to do with both God's initiative and human responsibility. God always takes the initiative in his relationship with us. We do not come to God or seek God on our own. "No one can come to Me unless the Father who sent Me draws him" (John 6:44). God is at work in our world calling people to repentance and relationship with him.

The reality is that not all people respond to God's invitation. Jewish teachers sometimes used parables as a way of separating diligent and lazy students.[1] In the same way, Jesus used his parables as a way of separating those whose hearts were—or were not—truly receptive to his message.

The "mysteries" Jesus referred to in verse 11 are not the same type of mystery as the latest bestselling book, but rather something secret that has now been revealed. Specifically, the reference is to the secret of God's redemptive work now fully revealed in Christ. Some understand these things, and some do not. Those who have a spiritual sensitivity that leads them to embrace Jesus' message are granted even more insight; those who have allowed their hearts to become hard experience continued hardening.

That some respond and some reject the message of Christ is a fulfillment of prophecy. Jesus quoted from Isaiah 6:9–10. Although the crowds all saw the same miracles and heard the same teachings from Jesus, some responded, but some rejected him. Those who rejected him heard the words but did not perceive the spiritual truth. They saw the miracles, but they didn't recognize that the miraculous signs pointed to the Savior now in their midst. The parables speak truth to those who want to hear it but are a judgment on the unbelief of those who have closed their hearts to the gospel.

A few months ago I was talking to a young woman who told me that she really wanted to know whether God was real. I encouraged her to pray, *God, if you're real, show me!* I suggested that if she spent a few minutes every day reading her Bible, asked God to speak to her, and was willing to do whatever God told her to do, God would reveal himself to her. She paused for a minute and then said, "You know, I don't really want to know that bad."

Real hunger makes itself known. Jesus' parables were understandable to his audience. In fact, Jesus' listeners by the Sea of Galilee most likely understood the parable of the sower more easily than we do today. Then as now, not all were willing to invest the time to consider his words and let them take root in their hearts. God said through the prophet Jeremiah, "You will seek Me and find Me when you search for Me with all your heart" (Jer. 29:13). Those who earnestly seek after God will find him, and those who open their hearts to God's message will be blessed (Matt. 13:16).

The Parable Explained (13:18–23)

Jesus explained to his disciples the meaning of the parable. The four types of soil represent four different responses to Jesus' message. Three types of soil do not produce fruitful plants, but the good soil produces a bountiful crop.

CASE STUDY

You have a friend who has faithfully served in your church's ministry to older children for the past year. She shares with you that she is increasingly frustrated and discouraged by the lack of response she sees. Although many seem interested in and receptive to the gospel, few of them ever make decisions. Often when the child gets to the point that he or she is asking questions and wanting to know more about Christ, his or her parents stop letting the child come. How can you encourage your friend?

The Road (13:18–19). Some seeds fall on the hardened path and are eaten by the birds before they have time to sprout. This type of soil represents those who hear the message but do not understand it because of their hardness of heart. Jesus says that for these people, "the evil one snatches away what has been sown in his heart" (13:18). Satan can either remove the truth from our minds or distort it if we give him an opening. Pharisees and other religious leaders of Jesus' time are examples of this type of listener. Although they heard the message of salvation just as the disciples did, most Pharisees rejected the truth without giving it a second thought.

*The Rocky Soil (13:20–21).*The seeds that fell on the shallow rocky soil grew up quickly. They were soon scorched by the sun and withered. The rocky soil represents those who appear to embrace the message of the gospel eagerly but quickly fall away once times of testing come. It may describe those who make an emotional decision rather than a true commitment of heart. Many of the crowds who followed Jesus would fall in this category. Although they eagerly responded to Jesus' miracles, they quickly deserted him when he challenged them with hard teachings or when persecution broke out (John 6:66). It is doubtful that this group really has true faith. When we present the gospel, we must be careful not to manipulate people's emotions. It is best to take the time to ensure a new believer is making a true commitment.

The Thorny Soil (13:22). The thorny soil is different from the first two in that the plants have an opportunity to grow. Although the seeds sprout, the plants have to compete so much for resources that they are choked out and never bear fruit. As Jesus explained, this soil represents one who hears and understands the gospel message, but "the worry of the world and the deceitfulness of wealth" keep him or her from fully committing to Christ. The rich young ruler is one example of this type of person (Matt. 19:16–26).

The Good Soil (13:23). The good soil represents the true followers of Christ, those who hear, understand, and receive the word so that it bears fruit in their lives. The test of time proves that these people have true faith. In fact, this is the only group we can clearly identify as having true saving faith. The emphasis is on this last group. Jesus' message to his disciples—and to us—is that the victory of the kingdom is sure. Many will reject the message of Christ for one reason or another, but some will respond. Those who do, have an amazing impact. Just as surely as seeds planted in good soil will sprout without human effort, the kingdom will surely come when the message of God is planted in receptive hearts. It is not a matter of luck, but of perseverance and commitment.

Implications and Actions

People respond to the gospel in different ways, and we do not have the privilege of knowing ahead of time how any given individual will respond. A pastor from India spoke to our church a few months ago. He shared with us that early in his ministry a group of men severely beat him, tied him to a tree, and left him for dead. Some of those same men are now leaders in his church.

Our responsibility is to preach the gospel to all people. We have the certain hope that some will respond. Today as in the first century, those who preach the message of Christ may face opposition. Yet we will also find that some will believe. We preach the word; God produces the harvest. In that hope, we can rejoice and celebrate.

QUESTIONS

1. Who in the Bible represents one of each of the four types of soil?

2. Thinking back on your faith journey, how did you initially respond to the gospel? What people or events helped you eventually make a commitment to Christ?

3. Do people respond to the gospel today in the same ways Jesus describes in this parable? How so?

4. How does this passage of Scripture help you deal with the reality that some people will not respond to the gospel?

5. How does this parable encourage you to share the gospel?

NOTES ───────────────────────────────────

1. M. Eugene Boring, "Matthew," *New Interpreter's Bible*, vol. VIII (Nashville: Abingdon, 1995), 304.

2. Timothy George, *Faithful Witness: The Life and Times of William Carey* (Birmingham: New Hope, 1991).

Hope in Jesus' Glorification

Hope is waiting to flood our lives as we consider the death and resurrection of Jesus Christ and the connection of Jesus' life with ours. We will have the opportunity through this unit to explore Matthew's perspective on hope from a universal, global, and all-encompassing view of the kingdom of God and our lives.

We have hope in the glorification of Jesus Christ, the Son of God. Just as God affirmed Jesus his Son in the transfiguration (Matthew 17:1–13; lesson 10), God affirms us in the purpose of our lives. God's affirmation of us through the life, death, burial, and resurrection of Jesus not only paves the way for us to have a meaningful life but also provides the responsibility to make disciples of Jesus and replicate the life and spirit of Christ in the lives of people in our circle of influence.

Lesson eleven points the way to a meaningful life through Jesus' crucifixion, and lesson twelve explores the calling of the Great Commission in light of our hope in the resurrected Christ.

The *bonus lesson* included in this study is titled "Jesus and Hurting People." It considers our responsibility to the poor, the needy, the sick, and the imprisoned among us.[1]

As I considered the Scripture passages for this unit, I was moved once again to the reality of Jesus in the world and in my own life and ministry. I hope the exploration of the Gospel of Matthew will awaken a drive in you to spend your life embracing the kingdom of God all around you.[2]

UNIT FOUR. HOPE IN JESUS' GLORIFICATION

NOTES

1. The bonus lesson is included because the time frame for the first use of this study has only twelve Sundays. However, to meet the needs of churches and classes who generally expect at least thirteen sessions in our studies, we have included a *bonus* lesson—"Jesus and Hurting People," on Matthew 25:31–46. If you study the bonus lesson, you may find it fits best after either lesson nine (because it is part of Jesus' teachings) or lesson ten (because the Scripture passages come after the passages in lesson ten in the Gospel of Matthew). You are encouraged to study it at some point because of the importance of its subject matter.

2. Unless otherwise indicated, all Scripture quotations in unit 4, lessons 10–12, and the bonus lesson are from the New International Version.

MAIN IDEA

In Jesus' transfiguration experience, God confirmed again that he was well pleased with Jesus, who would be crucified and then resurrected.

QUESTION TO EXPLORE

What does God's affirmation of Jesus' costly, selfless ministry mean for how we are to live?

STUDY AIM

To state what God's affirmation of Jesus in the transfiguration experience means for how I am to live

QUICK READ

God affirms his love for us and his call for our obedience to him through the example of Jesus' death and resurrection.

LESSON TEN
Affirmation of the Way of the Cross

105

Hardly anything is as exhilarating as receiving affirmation from a seasoned, respected, and proven leader. If you have had this privilege, you understand the sense of encouragement and challenge to do even better one feels when such affirmation comes. Perhaps it happened to you as a youth on an athletic team or in musical or other endeavors or later in your educational or work experience. Perhaps it occurred in your family in your growing-up years.

Shouldn't an affirming word from God mean even more to us considering the source? When you hear the affirming words of the Father to the Son and then to you, your life will be changed to his likeness. Having been in the light of God's presence, you will be more focused and determined to live out your mission for his sake.

MATTHEW 17:1–13

[1]After six days Jesus took with him Peter, James and John the brother of James, and led them up a high mountain by themselves. [2]There he was transfigured before them. His face shone like the sun, and his clothes became as white as the light. [3]Just then there appeared before them Moses and Elijah, talking with Jesus. [4]Peter said to Jesus, "Lord, it is good for us to be here. If you wish, I will put up three shelters—one for you, one for Moses and one for Elijah." [5]While he was still speaking, a bright cloud enveloped them, and a voice from the cloud said, "This is my Son, whom I love; with him I am well pleased. Listen to him!" [6]When the disciples heard this, they fell facedown to the ground, terrified. [7]But Jesus came and touched them. "Get up," he said. "Don't be afraid." [8]When they looked up, they saw no one except Jesus. [9]As they were coming down the mountain, Jesus instructed them, "Don't tell anyone what you have seen, until the Son of Man has been raised from the dead." [10]The disciples asked him, "Why then do the teachers of the law say that Elijah must come first?" [11]Jesus replied, "To be sure, Elijah comes and will restore all things. [12]But I tell you, Elijah has already come, and they did not recognize him, but have done to him everything they wished. In the same way the Son of Man is going to suffer at their hands." [13]Then the disciples understood that he was talking to them about John the Baptist.

From Parables to the Transfiguration (13:1—16:28)

Take a moment to scan Matthew 13—16 to become familiar with Jesus' teachings and actions leading up to the Transfiguration in Matthew 17. Note especially Matthew 16:13-28. There Jesus helped the disciples focus on his identity as the Son of Man—"the Christ, the Son of the Living God" (Matthew 16:16-17). He "began to explain to his disciples that he must go to Jerusalem and suffer many things . . . and that he must be killed and on the third day be raised to life" (Matt. 16:21). Jesus then pointedly described what being his follower meant: "If anyone would come after me, he must deny himself and take up his cross and follow me" (16:24).

Affirmation in the Inner Circle (17:1–4)

Have you ever had friends or colleagues close enough to you to find yourself in an inner circle of influence with them? Jesus had his inner circle of followers as well. They were Peter, James, and John the brother of James. Six days had passed since the experience at Caesarea Philippi in Matthew 16:13-28 when Jesus took his inner circle of followers up a high mountain.

Only the three disciples in Jesus' inner circle were with Jesus, indicating the special nature of this experience. The experience took place on a "high mountain," and thus was truly a mountaintop experience for these followers of Christ. One commentator suggests that the location of the mountain is Mount Tabor, a beautiful and isolated mountain that rises about 1,800 feet on the northeast part of the Plain of Esdraelon. Peter, James, and John would never forget this time with the Master.

When Jesus and his disciples reached the selected place, he was "transfigured" before their very eyes. What does this mean? The Gospel of Matthew says that Jesus' "face shone like the sun and his clothes became white as the light" (Matt. 17:2). The word for "transfigured" in New Testament Greek means *transformed* or *dramatically altered*. We might say Jesus underwent a metamorphosis in his appearance on the mountain in plain sight of his inner circle. Jesus, who had appeared in weakness and dishonor, was now appearing in power and glory to his followers.

At the very moment of Jesus' transfiguration, Moses and Elijah appeared and began talking with Jesus. Can you imagine what this would have been like? First, Peter, James, and John saw Jesus in his transfigured form, and then they saw Moses and Elijah join the occasion. What could this have meant for the inner circle? The appearance of Moses stood as a reminder of the Old Testament law, and the appearance of Elijah was a reminder of the work of the prophets. Both of them appearing at this moment bridged the old and the new covenants. The appearance of these two prominent Old Testament figures points to the unity of their work with the work of Jesus.

What an exhilarating experience it must have been while Moses, Elijah, and Jesus were in conversation! The appearance of Moses and Elijah conversing with Jesus was an affirmation of the work that lay before Jesus as he faced the cross (see Luke 9:31). Deuteronomy 18:15 says, "The Lord your God will raise up for you a prophet like me from among your own brothers. You must listen to him." Perhaps the appearance of Moses and Elijah focused the hearing of those in the inner circle on the things Jesus was teaching them in that experience.

Peter, James, and John must have scrambled for the slow-motion button in that mountaintop experience. They quickly came to the conclusion that it was good for them to be there, and they wanted the experience to last. Peter wanted to mark that place as holy ground by setting up three "shelters" (booths, tents) to preserve the moment.[1] The transfiguration, as understood by the inner circle, was a divine seal on the ministry of Jesus. This experience was further evidence that God was breaking through to the world through Christ. The transfiguration was also an affirmation of the faith of the disciples and an encouragement to worship.

Affirmation Advancing Mission (17:5–9)

While Peter was finishing his sentence related to setting up booths, a voice from a cloud said, "This is my Son, whom I love; with him I am well pleased. Listen to him!" As soon as the disciples heard these words, they fell facedown and were afraid. This was the second time during Jesus' ministry that he heard God's voice in affirmation. Matthew 3:17 says, "This is my Son, whom I love; with him I am well pleased." This first affirmation came at the baptism of Jesus by John. The second affirmation came as Jesus was preparing to conclude his earthly ministry. The voice of God pointed out the uniqueness of Jesus as God's Son and the uniqueness of Jesus' mission of redemption. These were affirming words spoken at just the right time.

The Gospel of Matthew records one phrase that is different from the affirmation at Jesus' baptism. Verse 5 concludes, "Listen to him!" Jesus immediately went to his disciples, touched them, and said, "Get up . . . don't be afraid." The disciples arose to find only Jesus standing with them. Once again Jesus instructed his disciples not to tell anyone what they had seen and heard until the resurrection.

The transfiguration experience centers redemption history in the person and work of Jesus. God's affirmation of Jesus in the presence of Jesus' followers strongly accentuated Jesus' authority for his disciples and for the church that would be birthed by his work. Jesus calmed the fears of his disciples, touching them with compassion. When they rose to their feet, they saw Jesus alone. Jesus was affirmed to advance his mission, and he, in turn, affirmed his inner circle of followers.

Affirmation Focused on Mission (17:10–13)

The disciples of the inner circle made an attempt to understand what they had just experienced by trying to sort out the life and ministry of

---

"NOT ONE ORPHAN BUT ALL ORPHANS . . ."

These words appear on the tombstone of Robert Cooke Buckner, founder of Buckner International. Even in post-Civil War Texas, Buckner, known as "Father" Buckner, had a clear and compelling mission: to serve all orphans. He was not satisfied with serving a few orphans but was focused on relentless pursuit of the well-being of all children living without families. In 1879 he called a Deacons Convention and challenged ordinary Baptist laypeople to fund a ministry to serve orphans in Texas. He placed the first two dollars in the hat he passed that day. That was the beginning of Buckner Children's Home in Dallas, Texas. R.C. Buckner's mission was to serve orphans. What is yours?

DOING KINGDOM MISSIONS

- You may want to consider conducting a shoe drive for children through Buckner's *Shoes for Orphan Souls*. See www.buckner.org for more information.

- You may want to consider serving as a mentor to a child in your community through KidsHope USA, a national program that matches a church member with one child for one hour a week in a local elementary school. See www.kidshopeusa.org.

- You may want to consider a family mission trip to serve children and families who are economically disadvantaged in your community or state.

- Reflect on your personal life mission and find a way to follow Jesus in serving among "the least of these" (Matt. 25:40).

Elijah. Jesus clearly stated that Elijah had come, but those to whom he came did not listen to him (see Malachi 4:5–6; Matt. 11:13–14).

Jesus then pointed to his impending death and the hope of his glory in completing his mission. In the background is the reality that John the Baptist—"the Elijah who was to come" (11:14)—had suffered too (see 14:1–12). In Matthew 16:24–26 Jesus stated that his disciples must take up their own cross and follow him. To save one's life means to lose it. The highest privilege is to know, accept, and fulfill one's God-given assignment. Jesus was ready to continue his mission of redemption.

Implications and Actions

God's affirmation of Jesus and of those who are called his disciples requires an obedient response to selfless living. Only through a passionate pursuit of our God-given mission do we really have the opportunity to live a meaningful life.

Jesus asked "What good will it be for a man if he gains the whole world, yet forfeits his soul? Or what can a man give in exchange for his soul?" (16:26). Living a life without redemptive meaning is like losing one's soul.

So what do we need for a meaningful life? Jesus alone is all we need for a meaningful life. We live so that we might hear the ultimate affirmation: "Well done, good and faithful servant!" (25:23).

QUESTIONS

1. How would you contrast the differences between people who really follow Jesus and those who are nominal to lukewarm in their devotion to Christ?

2. What is your personal life mission?

3. What are you doing with every day of life God gives you to advance your personal and redemptive mission?

4. Who, in your circle of influence, needs to hear an affirming word?

NOTES

1. Tents had been used to commemorate the experience of living in tents (or booths) during the Exodus under Moses' leadership (see Leviticus 23:42–43). The tabernacle, used in the same period, was also thought of as a tent.

FOCAL TEXT
Matthew 26:26–30;
27:11–14, 35–50

BACKGROUND
Matthew 26—27

MAIN IDEA
Jesus was faithful to his
mission to the point
of giving his life.

QUESTION TO EXPLORE
What does Jesus' giving his
life tell us about the kind
of disciples we are to be?

STUDY AIM
To decide how I will respond
to the message that the Son
of God gave his life for me

QUICK READ
Each one of us can choose
to live a meaningful or
meaningless life, a life with
or without eternal purpose.
Once you discover your
personal life mission, you have
something to live and die for.

LESSON ELEVEN
Giving His Life

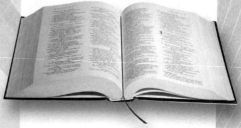

When I was in my early thirties, I attended a seminar that led me to begin to develop a life mission statement. I continue to use this life mission statement, in fact. My life mission statement is *to develop kingdom leaders from my circle of influence to the ends of the earth.* That statement has proved to be invaluable in guiding my life as well as how I use my time each day.

My experience is that developing such a statement will help a follower of Christ find his or her passion, mission, and vision; decide on what is worth his or her life; determine significant relationships needed to advance this mission; specify life tasks and goals; and take action in a focused, concentrated way so that one's life makes a difference. In this study, we will see that Jesus was fully faithful to his own mission, even to the point of giving his life.

MATTHEW 26:26–30

26While they were eating, Jesus took bread, gave thanks and broke it, and gave it to his disciples, saying, "Take and eat; this is my body."

27Then he took the cup, gave thanks and offered it to them, saying, "Drink from it, all of you. 28This is my blood of the covenant, which is poured out for many for the forgiveness of sins. 29I tell you, I will not drink of this fruit of the vine from now on until that day when I drink it anew with you in my Father's kingdom."

30When they had sung a hymn, they went out to the Mount of Olives.

MATTHEW 27:11–14, 35–50

11Meanwhile Jesus stood before the governor, and the governor asked him, "Are you the king of the Jews?"

"Yes, it is as you say," Jesus replied.

12When he was accused by the chief priests and the elders, he gave no answer. 13Then Pilate asked him, "Don't you hear the testimony they are bringing against you?" 14But Jesus made no reply, not even to a single charge—to the great amazement of the governor.

. . . .

³⁵When they had crucified him, they divided up his clothes by casting lots. ³⁶And sitting down, they kept watch over him there. ³⁷Above his head they placed the written charge against him: THIS IS JESUS, THE KING OF THE JEWS. ³⁸Two robbers were crucified with him, one on his right and one on his left. ³⁹Those who passed by hurled insults at him, shaking their heads ⁴⁰and saying, "You who are going to destroy the temple and build it in three days, save yourself! Come down from the cross, if you are the Son of God!"

⁴¹In the same way the chief priests, the teachers of the law and the elders mocked him. ⁴²"He saved others," they said, "but he can't save himself! He's the King of Israel! Let him come down now from the cross, and we will believe in him. ⁴³He trusts in God. Let God rescue him now if he wants him, for he said, 'I am the Son of God.' " ⁴⁴In the same way the robbers who were crucified with him also heaped insults on him.

⁴⁵From the sixth hour until the ninth hour darkness came over all the land. ⁴⁶About the ninth hour Jesus cried out in a loud voice, *"Eloi, Eloi, lama sabachthani?"*—which means, "My God, my God, why have you forsaken me?"

⁴⁷When some of those standing there heard this, they said, "He's calling Elijah."

⁴⁸Immediately one of them ran and got a sponge. He filled it with wine vinegar, put it on a stick, and offered it to Jesus to drink. ⁴⁹The rest said, "Now leave him alone. Let's see if Elijah comes to save him."

⁵⁰And when Jesus had cried out again in a loud voice, he gave up his spirit.

Mission Possible (26:26–30)

In the previous lesson, on Matthew 17:1–13, Jesus took his disciples up a high mountain to be alone with them and to be transfigured before their very eyes. Jesus was attempting to help the disciples understand that his mission was to die for those he loved. His mission was redemption, and he was willing to die for it. In Matthew 26:26–30 we fast-forward the story to the celebration of the Last Supper. At this time, Jesus would show his followers, through the celebration of the Supper, what it would mean to give his life as a ransom for many.

The journey to this point had been filled with potential distractions. For example, in Matthew 4:1–11, the Gospel writer shows us how Jesus was able to say *no* to the invitations of the devil in the wilderness. Too, in Matthew 17:4 Peter suggested that tents be set up for Jesus, Moses, and Elijah so they could remain in that moment.

Once you find your life's mission, the distractions seem to multiply. Even good things can become attempts to keep one from what is best. Being faithful to one's mission requires the best focus and determination to overcome temptation and stay on task. The father of all lies would have you believe that your mission is really a mission impossible. At the Last Supper Jesus showed us how to live by showing us how to die with purpose.

The Last Supper was celebrated with bread and wine, common elements at a Jewish meal. Jesus assigned a special meaning to the bread and wine on this occasion. To the bread, a thin sheet of unleavened bread, he assigned the symbolic value of his body that was to be broken. To the wine he assigned the symbolic value of his blood that was to be shed as a ransom for those who would believe. In Matthew 26:28 Jesus said, "This is my blood of the covenant, which is poured out for many for the forgiveness of sins."

The "covenant" to which Jesus referred was like a will and testament. The result of the pouring out of Christ's blood through his death was that followers of Christ would now have the inheritance as God's heirs, joint-heirs with Christ. All the blessings found in Christ would now belong to those who became his disciples. The testament of Christ's death on the cross was connected to Jesus' followers by his blood that was shed.

Included in the biblical background for the idea of "covenant" was the covenant God made with Moses at Mount Sinai in Exodus 24:4–8. This covenant was sealed with the blood of oxen thrown upon the altar, symbolizing the bond between God and Israel. Too, Jeremiah 31:31–34 says that the covenant would no longer be written on tablets but would be written on the hearts of people who come to know God in the forgiveness of sins. The blood to which Jesus referred inaugurated the new covenant with God's people.

MISSION TO THE LEAST OF THESE

By one estimate, there are 143 million orphans in the world today. Too, approximately 1.5 million children roam the streets of Mexico City, and about 300,000 of them are truly abandoned children. Further, about 500,000 children are in foster care in the United States. Can we not do something about this? What if each congregation helped one family adopt one child?

Jesus told his disciples to bring the children to him so he might bless them rather than keep them out of sight and out of mind (Matt. 19:13–15). Our churches are in a position to do the same. Isn't this how our crucified and risen King would have us live? James said, "Religion that God our Father accepts as pure and faultless is this: to look after orphans and widows in their distress and to keep oneself from being polluted by the world" (James 1:27).

Jesus' blood shed for us is the marker of his mission in our lives. Through Jesus' shed blood we have the possibility of the forgiveness of our sins and of a life filled with purpose.

Mission Examined (27:11–14)

You have heard this phrase before: *Silence is golden.* The silence of Jesus while he stood accused before Pilate was deafening. Pilate asked Jesus, "Are you the king of the Jews?" Jesus' answer, "Yes, it is as you say," was meant to confirm the contents of Pilate's question, but Jesus was not saying that he was a political leader. He was and is more. Pilate's examination of Jesus and his mission did not keep Jesus from his ultimate goal.

In Pilate's second wave of interrogation, he asked Jesus whether he had heard the accusations of the chief priests and the elders. Jesus, though, made no reply to a single charge. Pilate was in great amazement at Jesus' lack of self-defense.

Pilate may well have had only two choices—to silence Jesus' angry accusers or to investigate the charges. He chose not to pursue either route and tried to place this responsibility on the accused. Jesus' silence,

---

YOUR MISSION?

Take some time to think about what your mission in life is. Write it down, and consider what you need to do to follow it.

---

however, did not dignify the accusations with a response. Sometimes providing an answer to an accusation only encourages the accuser. Pilate never judged Jesus as being guilty of the accusations against him and remained puzzled about the strength Jesus displayed in the face of death. Pilate could see that Jesus was no ordinary prisoner.

On many occasions, I have found there to be great power in silence. Sometimes I think we talk too much and don't say anything at all. Jesus remained silent in the face of false accusations and in so doing spoke volumes about his mission and his purpose in redemption. On the outside it looked like human beings were shaping events, but in reality Jesus was working his purpose through this whole experience. Jesus' commitment to our redemption, to the cross, and to the will of his Father could not be swayed even with the opportunity to defend himself against false accusations. He was focused on his mission.

Results Worth Your Life (27:35–50)

What results are worth your life? In other words, what results would be worth your laying down your life so that this goal could be achieved?

Jesus knew the answers to these questions. He gave his life so that we might live. From his perspective, our redemption and forgiveness was worth his life. Jesus loved us so much that he was obedient even to death on a cross to save us from our own destructiveness.

Jesus was able to maintain absolute focus on his mission through his death even as soldiers gambled over his clothes, as the men who were crucified with him mocked and hurled insults at him, and even as the chief priests, the teachers of the law, and the elders came by to insult and mock him as well. While Matthew records both thieves insulting Jesus, Luke 23:32–43 records that one of the thieves repented of his sin and recognized Jesus as the Son of God.

After three hours of darkness, Jesus cried out these words in a loud voice: *"Eloi, Eloi, lama sabachthani?"* Matthew said these words meant, "My God, My God, why have you forsaken me?" Why did Jesus utter them? These words from Psalm 22 expressed Jesus' sense of abandonment. Note, though, that in spite of the depth of his suffering, Jesus was still praying to God the Father. Even in Jesus' loneliest moment, as he bore the sins of the world, there was a nearness to God. God was at the same time distant and present.

When we feel we have been abandoned, God is near. When we feel we have been treated unjustly, we can still ask God *why.* We may not hear God's response, but we can be sure that God hears and is near.

One of the people observing the crucifixion brought Jesus a mixture of wine and vinegar for him to drink. Others continued mocking him and waiting to see whether Elijah would come to Jesus' aid. This did not deter Jesus from his mission. After this he cried out with a loud voice and died. This last act fulfilled a number of scriptural references in Matthew that pointed to the death of Jesus. Matthew 16:21; 17:12, 22; and 20:18 all point to the death of Jesus.

Jesus breathed his last breath and then died. He acted as the sovereign Lord even in his death. He chose voluntarily to die at that moment. With that final act of his will, Jesus completed his mission.

GO, BE, DO

- Consider being the presence of Christ in the lives of children at risk in your community, state, nation, or across the seas. You may want to look into becoming a foster care parent to provide a home for a child even on a temporary basis. Check with local possibilities, call Buckner International at 214–758–8000, or see www.buckner.org for more information.

- Consider doing something this year that will meet the needs of a child at risk. You might consider volunteering at a local after-school program or going on a mission trip to serve children in Mexico, Guatemala, Peru, Honduras, Ethiopia, Kenya, Russia, Romania, or Latvia. One way to find an opportunity is at www.itsyourmission.org.

Implications and Actions

Jesus taught us both how to live and how to die. He taught us how to live life to its fullest with robust purpose and mission. He taught us how to obey even to death for the things we are called to pursue. This kind of living and dying should help us know how we should live our lives—and how we should think about death.

In what way does Jesus' death help us shape how we are going to live? Followers of Jesus need to know their life mission and then live it out to the fullest. I would rather live my life with lots of risk so I might pursue that which God has called me to do rather than live a safe life of meaninglessness.

Jesus lived out his mission and died to free us from the consequences of our sin. What is *your* mission? Have you found what you are willing to die for?

QUESTIONS

1. Do you have a personal life mission, a mission big enough to live for? to die for?

2. What results are worth your life?

3. When have you found it best to remain silent when falsely accused?

4. How do you handle the feeling of being abandoned, even by God? What does Jesus' experience teach us?

LESSON TWELVE
Under the Command of the Resurrected Christ

Many church leaders today have serious concerns about how well our churches are doing in truly making disciples of Jesus. A church known and respected for its efforts in seeking innovative ways in carrying out Jesus' mission did a serious assessment of their discipleship efforts. The church found that a significant percentage of its members felt their spiritual growth was stalled and indeed were dissatisfied with church. The church's leaders came to the conclusion that the church was not doing a good job of truly leading people to become followers of Christ even though many people attended. What about your church? What about you?

The focus of this lesson is on making disciples. Let's go back to the source to see what Jesus meant when he told his followers they were to make disciples of all nations.

MATTHEW 28:1–10, 16–20

¹After the Sabbath, at dawn on the first day of the week, Mary Magdalene and the other Mary went to look at the tomb.

²There was a violent earthquake, for an angel of the Lord came down from heaven and, going to the tomb, rolled back the stone and sat on it. ³His appearance was like lightning, and his clothes were white as snow. ⁴The guards were so afraid of him that they shook and became like dead men.

⁵The angel said to the women, "Do not be afraid, for I know that you are looking for Jesus, who was crucified. ⁶He is not here; he has risen, just as he said. Come and see the place where he lay. ⁷Then go quickly and tell his disciples: 'He has risen from the dead and is going ahead of you into Galilee. There you will see him.' Now I have told you."

⁸So the women hurried away from the tomb, afraid yet filled with joy, and ran to tell his disciples. ⁹Suddenly Jesus met them. "Greetings," he said. They came to him, clasped his feet and worshiped him. ¹⁰Then Jesus said to them, "Do not be afraid. Go and tell my brothers to go to Galilee; there they will see me."

*   *   *   *   *   *   *   *   *   *   *   *   *   *   *   *

¹⁶Then the eleven disciples went to Galilee, to the mountain where Jesus had told them to go. ¹⁷When they saw him, they

worshiped him; but some doubted. [18]Then Jesus came to them and said, "All authority in heaven and on earth has been given to me. [19]Therefore go and make disciples of all nations, baptizing them in the name of the Father and of the Son and of the Holy Spirit, [20]and teaching them to obey everything I have commanded you. And surely I am with you always, to the very end of the age."

The Context for Making Disciples (28:1–10)

It is critical to recall that the context for the instructions in the Great Commission to make disciples of all nations was the resurrection of Jesus. The One who commanded his followers to make disciples of all nations was the resurrected Lord, who appeared to his disciples with wounds in his hands and side.

Note carefully that the first followers to whom Jesus appeared were "Mary Magdalene and the other Mary" (Matthew 28:1). Mary Magdalene was the woman who had been possessed by demons and was freed by Jesus (Luke 8:2). The "other Mary" most likely refers to "the mother of James and Joses" (Matt. 27:56), identified by church tradition as the sister of Mary the mother of Jesus.

The two women likely went to the tomb to finish work on Jesus' body. Those who came to serve the Servant who gave his life were women and were the first ones to learn that the tomb was empty and Jesus had risen from the dead.

Right at the time of the arrival of the women at the tomb, a violent earthquake occurred, "for an angel of the Lord came down from heaven" (28:2). The angel went "to the tomb, rolled back the stone and sat on it" (28:2). The angel's "appearance was like lightning, and his clothes were as white as snow." The angel's appearance so frightened the guards that "they shook and became like dead men" (28:4).

The angel, though, told the women not to be afraid, for he knew they were looking for Jesus. The angel continued, "He is not here; he has risen, just as he said. Come and see the place where he lay. Then go quickly and tell his disciples: 'He has risen from the dead and is going ahead of you into Galilee. There you will see him.'" Before Jesus' death he had promised a meeting in Galilee (26:32). Matthew 28:16 records that meeting.

Worship and Discipleship (28:16–18)

The stage was set for a dramatic meeting between Jesus' disciples and Jesus in Galilee. There Jesus appeared to them, and they began to worship him. The disciples' reasons for worshiping Jesus related to recognizing it was him but also to believing in their hearts that he was the Son of God and all that he had said about himself had come true. Matthew also records that some of the disciples "doubted."

Jesus knew the disciples' hearts and immediately spoke to settle any doubts, thus positioning himself to give his final instructions. He said that all authority in heaven and earth was his. God had given him comprehensive authority over the created order. Based on this authority, Jesus would instruct, empower, and inspire confidence in his disciples to make disciples throughout the world.

Our authority for making disciples comes from Jesus. When we recognize Jesus for who he is, we worship him and are ready to make disciples. I believe there is a connection between worship and making disciples. If we do not truly worship, will we be willing and able to make disciples?

Discipleship: Baptizing and Teaching Them to Obey (28:19–20)

The bridge between Jesus' authority and the task of making disciples is found in the word "therefore" (Matt. 28:19). This word links the previous discussion with the commission Jesus gave in verses 19–20. "Make disciples" is the central verb, the main focus of the commission. "Make disciples" is the command. The arena in which we are to "make disciples" is throughout the world since the object of making disciples is "all nations."

The two actions in the process of making disciples are "baptizing" and "teaching." In the first century, baptism was a religious rite that indicated a cleansing of the heart. Too, for followers of Jesus, it was a public demonstration of identity with Christ, a public affirmation that the baptized person was unmistakably identified with him. Baptism was to be "in the name of the Father and of the Son and of the Holy Spirit." This is one of the earliest known uses of the Trinitarian formula.

The other crucial action in the process of making disciples is "teaching." The word "disciples" means *learners* or *pupils*. The emphasis of the

How to Apply This Lesson

- Review the life of Jesus, and decide to imitate or follow him in everything you do.
- Look for life applications in each Bible study you read, each lesson you experience, and each sermon you hear.
- Be the presence of Christ in the life of another person around you.
- Share the good news of the gospel with a family member, neighbor, coworker, or friend. Then decide to start the adventure of teaching that person to obey everything Jesus commanded.
- Look for ways to disciple the children or grandchildren in your life.

Great Commission is not on the announcement of the gospel news as much as it is on the task of teaching those who respond to obey.

Discipleship is teaching followers of Jesus to obey everything Jesus commanded. That is the heart of making disciples. What we are to teach is obedience and not only content. We are to teach followers of Jesus how to obey. This implies a submission to the authority of Jesus, the one who said, "All authority in heaven and on earth has been given to me" (28:18). Followers of Jesus are to teach everything Jesus commanded. The emphasis of "teaching them to obey everything I have commanded" is not on doctrine but on actual obedience to Jesus' commands.

So how do we teach a follower of Jesus to obey everything Jesus commanded? Obviously instruction is needed. How do we provide instruction? Certainly many followers of Jesus get instruction through preaching, Bible study, and similar means. Few, however, get practical experience, demonstration, and mentoring in the Christian life. This is hard to do in large groups or crowds and much more practical when practiced person to person, one on one, or in small groups. Jesus showed the Twelve how to live, and then he pulled in an inner circle of three so he could mentor them more personally.

Implications and Actions

My observation is that most churches tend to major on the propositional content of Jesus' teaching rather than on calling for practical application in life. However, if "teaching them to obey everything" Jesus commanded is to be a reality, then our focus needs to change. The aim must be not merely saying *I believe* or even accumulating knowledge but becoming people who live Jesus' way.

QUESTIONS

1. Do you think we emphasize the "make disciples" part of the Great Commission as much as we need to?

2. What would have to change about your life for you to follow more faithfully Jesus' command to "make disciples"?

3. What would have to change about your church for it to follow more faithfully Jesus' command to "make disciples"?

4. If your church's mission is making disciples, what criteria should be used to identify this mission as accomplished?

FOCAL TEXT
Matthew 25:31–46

BACKGROUND
Matthew 25:31–46

MAIN IDEA
The exalted Son of Man demonstrates concern for the lowliest and neediest of people and demands that his followers do the same.

QUESTION TO EXPLORE
Helping hungry, thirsty, poorly-clothed, sick, imprisoned people is just an option, isn't it?

STUDY AIM
To decide on ways I will prepare for the final examination

QUICK READ
Authentic disciples of Jesus Christ feed the hungry, give water to the thirsty, provide clothes to the poorly dressed, help the sick, and serve imprisoned people. Engaging in such actions is not an option for Christians.

BONUS LESSON
Jesus and Hurting People

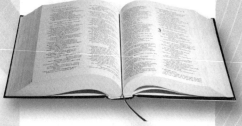

Shortly after I had become president of the Baptist General Convention of Texas a few years ago, I had opportunity to speak to a group of Baptist leaders. I chose to challenge the group to emphasize what I call a *Jesus agenda* that year. So I decided to base my message on the passage in Luke 4 in which Jesus challenged the people in the synagogue at Nazareth, saying: "The Spirit of the Lord is upon me, because he has anointed me to bring good news to the poor. He has sent me to proclaim release to the captives and recovery of sight to the blind, to let the oppressed go free, to proclaim the year of the Lord's favor" (Luke 4:18–19). In my message, I pointed out the various elements of Jesus' ministry. The group received my message enthusiastically, with a solid round of *amens*. I felt I had made a good impression for my first presentation that year, but I was not prepared for what would happen next.

Later that year in a spiritual retreat, I was led to begin thinking more about the *Jesus agenda*. I could not get this topic off my mind. My message went from a good rally cry that received *amens* to a challenge that penetrated my heart. I could not stop thinking about what Jesus meant by preaching "good news to the poor." I came to a crisis of faith about my personal involvement on behalf of the poor.

Little did I know that this passion that was growing in me would lead me to consider a post as president of Buckner Children and Family Services, Inc. Beginning January of 2007 I started serving in this role to focus on the needs of 143 million orphans and children at risk around the world through the ministry of Buckner International (www.buckner.org).

I pray that this lesson will move you toward the poor, the thirsty, the poorly-clothed, the sick, and the prisoner—the people in need whom Jesus said we would help if we were his followers. Following the risen Christ authentically will lead you to "the least of these" (Matthew 25:40).

In the Background

Matthew 17:14 through 24:30 provides the broad context for this lesson. Matthew 17:14–23 records the healing of a boy with a demon after Jesus' transfiguration (see lesson 10). Toward the end of that chapter, Jesus responded to a question about paying taxes.

Chapter 18 contains the fourth major block of Jesus' teachings in Matthew (see Matt. 5—7; 10; 13; 18; 23—25). There Jesus taught about the need to "welcome" children, followed by teachings on forgiveness and reconciliation.

Matthew 19 records Jesus' teaching on divorce, an incident in which Jesus taught further about the place of children, and then Jesus' encounter with the rich young man. Chapter 20 contains additional teachings in parables and Jesus' response to the question of the mother of James and John. Matthew 21—22 includes Jesus' triumphal entry, his cleansing the temple, and additional parables. Matthew 23—25 is the final major block of Jesus' teachings in Matthew.

MATTHEW 25:31–46

[31]"When the Son of Man comes in his glory, and all the angels with him, he will sit on his throne in heavenly glory. [32]All the nations will be gathered before him, and he will separate the people one from another as a shepherd separates the sheep from the goats. [33]He will put the sheep on his right and the goats on his left.

[34]"Then the King will say to those on his right, 'Come, you who are blessed by my Father; take your inheritance, the kingdom prepared for you since the creation of the world. [35]For I was hungry and you gave me something to eat, I was thirsty and you gave me something to drink, I was a stranger and you invited me in, [36]I needed clothes and you clothed me, I was sick and you looked after me, I was in prison and you came to visit me.'

[37]"Then the righteous will answer him, 'Lord, when did we see you hungry and feed you, or thirsty and give you something to drink? [38]When did we see you a stranger and invite you in, or needing clothes and clothe you? [39]When did we see you sick or in prison and go to visit you?'

[40]"The King will reply, 'I tell you the truth, whatever you did for one of the least of these brothers of mine, you did for me.'

[41]"Then he will say to those on his left, 'Depart from me, you who are cursed, into the eternal fire prepared for the devil and his angels. [42]For I was hungry and you gave me nothing to eat, I was

thirsty and you gave me nothing to drink, ⁴³I was a stranger and you did not invite me in, I needed clothes and you did not clothe me, I was sick and in prison and you did not look after me.'

⁴⁴"They also will answer, 'Lord, when did we see you hungry or thirsty or a stranger or needing clothes or sick or in prison, and did not help you?'

⁴⁵"He will reply, 'I tell you the truth, whatever you did not do for one of the least of these, you did not do for me.'

⁴⁶"Then they will go away to eternal punishment, but the righteous to eternal life."

Judgment Teaching: The Sheep and the Goats (25:31–33)

In this passage, Jesus used a metaphor of sheep and goats to teach about the marks of authenticity in those who call themselves his followers. This passage is not referred to as a parable, and so it is best not to call it that. It is always best not to ascribe to the Scripture what it does not ascribe for itself.

Jesus' teachings in this passage are about the final judgment. Jesus described the Son of Man coming with angels at the end of time to sit on a judgment throne. All the nations will be before him, and he will begin separating them "as a shepherd separates the sheep from the goats" (25:32).

The phrase "the nations" in New Testament Greek is *panta ta ethne.* Some commentators interpret this phrase to refer to the Gentiles, but that interpretation does not seem best. Jesus used these same words in the Great Commission in Matthew 28:19–20. The words thus refer to all the nations of the world. So the meaning is that all the people from every tribe and every nation will be gathered at the end of time around the judgment throne. In Matthew's mind, Jesus was King over the whole world and was exercising his authority as such.

Shepherds could easily distinguish sheep and goats. Using the image of separating sheep from goats, Jesus taught that the sheep would be placed on the right and the goats on the left. In the culture of that day, the right hand side was reserved as the place of honor. Goats were sent to the left side of the throne, the side of condemnation. While we are taught by Jesus not to judge others (see Matt. 7:1), we see that Jesus has this right and place because he is God. He is the King of kings and someday will sit on his throne to judge all the people from all the nations of the earth.

Matthew's use of the terminology of the Son of Man implies judgment, as we see in Jesus' use of this phrase in Matthew 19:28 and 24:30. In these instances Matthew is referring to the end of the age when the Son of Man is seated on his throne in his glory.[1] The Son of Man comes to judge the world and to discern those who are his.

The Way of the Sheep (25:34–40)

Jesus teaches in this passage that the King of heaven will gladly welcome his sheep into the place he has prepared for them. Then Jesus spells out the criteria by which he is making this decision or judgment. The evidence that the sheep belong to Jesus is as follows: they provide food, water, hospitality, clothes, and care for the sick and the prisoner.

Recall again Jesus' inaugural message in Luke 4:17–19. Have you ever thought about how that passage in which Jesus outlined his agenda for ministry relates to this passage? I confess that I hadn't before my own spiritual experience mentioned at the beginning of this lesson. Note, though, that in Luke 4:17–19 Jesus said he was going to serve the poor, the prisoners, the blind, and the oppressed and to tell about God's favor. Jesus' outline of his agenda for ministry in Luke 4 reminds me pointedly of Jesus' standards for judgment in Matthew 25:34–30, In other words, Jesus outlined his agenda for his ministry and will judge people by it in order to qualify those who really belong to him.

A WAY TO SERVE JESUS BY SERVING PEOPLE

Buckner International (see www.buckner.org) serves orphans, children at risk, and families in fourteen Texas cities, Oklahoma, Washington, and Tennessee as well as eight countries beyond the United States, including Mexico, Guatemala, Peru, Russia, Romania, Latvia, Ethiopia, and Kenya. We send humanitarian aid in the form of shoes to more than sixty nations and collect about 200,000 pairs of shoes through *Shoes for Orphan Souls* each year. We exist to serve the least of these and to provide a way for you to serve them too.

Note that the standard in Matthew 25:31–46 for testing authenticity at the judgment is not the content of one's beliefs, or theological knowledge. Jesus is not interested in intellectual assent to the claims of the gospel. What Jesus uses to measure authenticity is the kind of actions he announced at the beginning of his ministry. This teaching agrees with James's teaching regarding not merely hearing the word but doing something about it as well (see James 1:22). Note, too, though, that Jesus is not teaching that doing good works is the way to earn salvation at the judgment. Rather, Jesus is emphasizing that if a person is a disciple he or she will focus on helping the people who matter to Jesus.

Authentic followers of Jesus Christ feed the hungry, give water to the thirsty, provide clothes to the poorly dressed, help the sick, and serve imprisoned people. They do these things because of a personal relationship with Christ and not in an effort to earn favor. Our serving the least of these and imitating Jesus through those opportunities brings him great joy.

Those who served the hungry, the thirsty, the poor, the sick, and the prisoner could not remember when they had served the King in this way. Jesus clarified that when we serve people in this way we are actually serving Christ. The King says, ". . . whatever you did for one of the least these brothers of mine, you did for me" (Matt. 25:40).

The Way of the Goats (25:41–46)

The way of the goats is one of rejection from the heavenly reward and fellowship with the King. The King says to those on his left that they are "cursed," sending them "into the eternal fire prepared for the devil and his angels" (25:41). The people on his left were confused because they did not know when they did not provide for the various needs of the King, the Lord. The King pointed out, "I tell you the truth, whatever you did not do for one of the least of these, you did not do for me" (25:45).

In this passage, Jesus thus shows his identification with people with various kinds of needs. He calls us to serve them because in so doing we serve him.

HOW TO APPLY THIS LESSON

- Go to a place in your community, county, state, elsewhere in your country, or across the seas to serve the least of these.
- Get involved in a ministry to prisoners in your county or state detention center.
- Give time, money, or food to your local food bank.
- Donate a pair of new shoes for the *Shoes for Orphan Souls* program (www.buckner.org).

Implications and Actions

I live with one question that makes me get up in the morning. I ask this question of myself in light of the estimated 143 million orphans in the world today; 1.5 million children at risk on the streets in Mexico City; 300,000 abandoned children with no parental support or supervision on the streets of Mexico City; and 500,000 children in foster care and waiting to be adopted in the United States. In addition, most American Christians struggle to decide what kind of food they want to eat for lunch while most of the developing world may eat only once a day.

Here is the question: *How much longer will a just God allow American Christians to have most of the world's wealth and resources while the rest of the developing world has next to nothing?*

QUESTIONS

1. In what ways would you be willing to serve the needy, the sick, and those in prison?

2. What prevents you from going to the poorest places in the world to serve "the least of these" (25:45)?

3. What would it take for you to manage your resources so you could provide financial resources to those who are less fortunate?

4. How would you have to adjust your schedule in order to have time to serve the poor, the sick, the prisoner, the hungry, and the oppressed?

NOTES ───────────────────────────────────────

1. See also Daniel 7:13–14; 2 Thessalonians 1:7–10; John 5:27.

Our Next New Study
(Available for use beginning March 2009)

EZRA, HAGGAI, ZECHARIAH, NEHEMIAH, MALACHI: Restoring the Future

Additional Resources for Studying Ezra, Haggai, Zechariah, Nehemiah, Malachi: Restoring the Future [1]

EZRA

Emmett Willard Hamrick. "Ezra—Nehemiah." *The Broadman Bible Commentary*. Volume 3. Nashville, Tennessee: Broadman Press, 1970.

Ralph W. Klein. "The Books of Ezra & Nehemiah." *The New Interpreter's Bible*. Volume III. Nashville: Abingdon Press, 1999.

H. G. M. Williamson. "Ezra-Nehemiah." *Word Biblical Commentary*. Volume 16, Waco, TX: Word Books, 1985.

HAGGAI

W. Eugene March. "Haggai." *The New Interpreter's Bible*. Volume VII. Nashville: Abingdon Press, 1996.

Paul L. Redditt. *Haggai, Zechariah, and Malachi*. New Century Bible Commentary. Grand Rapids, Michigan: Eerdmans, 1994.

David A. Smith. "Haggai." *The Broadman Bible Commentary*. Volume 7. Nashville, Tennessee: Broadman Press, 1972.

Ralph L. Smith. "Haggai." *Word Biblical Commentary*. Volume 32. Waco, Texas: Word Books, Publisher, 1984.

ZECHARIAH

Ben C. Ollenburger. "Zechariah." *The New Interpreter's Bible*. Volume VII. Nashville: Abingdon Press, 1996.

Paul L. Redditt. *Haggai, Zechariah, and Malachi*. New Century Bible Commentary. Grand Rapids, Michigan: Eerdmans, 1994.

John D. W. Watts. "Zechariah." *The Broadman Bible Commentary*. Volume 7. Nashville, Tennessee: Broadman Press, 1972.

NEHEMIAH

Emmett Willard Hamrick. "Ezra—Nehemiah." *The Broadman Bible Commentary.* Volume 3. Nashville, Tennessee: Broadman Press, 1970.

Ralph W. Klein. "The Books of Ezra & Nehemiah." *The New Interpreter's Bible.* Volume III. Nashville: Abingdon Press, 1999.

Charles R. Swindoll. *Hand Me Another Brick.* New York: Bantam Books, 1978.

MALACHI

T. Miles Bennett. "Malachi." *The Broadman Bible Commentary.* Volume 7. Nashville, Tennessee: Broadman Press, 1972.

Page H. Kelley. *Malachi: Rekindling the Fires of Faith.* Nashville, Tennessee: Convention Press, 1986.

Paul L. Redditt. *Haggai, Zechariah, and Malachi.* New Century Bible Commentary. Grand Rapids, Michigan: Eerdmans, 1994.

Eileen M. Schuller. "Malachi." *The New Interpreter's Bible.* Volume VII. Nashville: Abingdon Press, 1996.

Additional Future Adult Studies

Participating in God's Mission	For use beginning June 2009
Galatians and Thessalonians: Building on a Solid Foundation	For use beginning September 2009
The Gospel of Luke	For use beginning December 2009

NOTES ——————————————————————

1. Listing a book does not imply full agreement by the writers or BAPTISTWAY PRESS® with all of its comments.

How to Order More Bible Study Materials

It's easy! Just fill in the following information. For additional Bible study materials, see www.baptistwaypress.org or get a complete order form of available materials by calling 1-866-249-1799 or e-mailing baptistway@bgct.org.

Title of item	Price	Quantity	Cost
This Issue:			
Matthew: Hope in the Resurrected Christ—Study Guide (BWP001066)	$3.25	_____	_____
Matthew: Hope in the Resurrected Christ—Large Print Study Guide (BWP001067)	$3.55	_____	_____
Matthew: Hope in the Resurrected Christ—Teaching Guide (BWP001068)	$3.75	_____	_____
Additional Issues Available:			
Growing Together in Christ—Study Guide (BWP001036)	$3.25	_____	_____
Growing Together in Christ—Large Print Study Guide (BWP001037)	$3.55	_____	_____
Growing Together in Christ—Teaching Guide (BWP001038)	$3.75	_____	_____
Genesis 12—50: Family Matters—Study Guide (BWP000034)	$1.95	_____	_____
Genesis 12—50: Family Matters—Teaching Guide (BWP000035)	$2.45	_____	_____
Leviticus, Numbers, Deuteronomy—Study Guide (BWP000053)	$2.35	_____	_____
Leviticus, Numbers, Deuteronomy—Large Print Study Guide (BWP000052)	$2.35	_____	_____
Leviticus, Numbers, Deuteronomy—Teaching Guide (BWP000054)	$2.95	_____	_____
Joshua, Judges—Study Guide (BWP000047)	$2.35	_____	_____
Joshua, Judges—Large Print Study Guide (BWP000046)	$2.35	_____	_____
Joshua, Judges—Teaching Guide (BWP000048)	$2.95	_____	_____
1 and 2 Samuel—Study Guide (BWP000002)	$2.35	_____	_____
1 and 2 Samuel—Large Print Study Guide (BWP000001)	$2.35	_____	_____
1 and 2 Samuel—Teaching Guide (BWP000003)	$2.95	_____	_____
1 and 2 Kings: Leaders and Followers—Study Guide (BWP001025)	$2.95	_____	_____
1 and 2 Kings: Leaders and Followers Large Print Study Guide (BWP001026)	$3.15	_____	_____
1 and 2 Kings: Leaders and Followers Teaching Guide (BWP001027)	$3.45	_____	_____
Job, Ecclesiastes, Habakkuk, Lamentations: Dealing with Hard Times—Study Guide (BWP001016)	$2.75	_____	_____
Job, Ecclesiastes, Habakkuk, Lamentations: Dealing with Hard Times—Large Print Study Guide (BWP001017)	$2.85	_____	_____
Job, Ecclesiastes, Habakkuk, Lamentations: Dealing with Hard Times—Teaching Guide (BWP001018)	$3.25	_____	_____
Psalms and Proverbs: Songs and Sayings of Faith— Study Guide (BWP001000)	$2.75	_____	_____
Psalms and Proverbs: Songs and Sayings of Faith— Large Print Study Guide (BWP001001)	$2.85	_____	_____
Psalms and Proverbs: Songs and Sayings of Faith— Teaching Guide (BWP001002)	$3.25	_____	_____
Mark: Jesus' Works and Words—Study Guide (BWP001022)	$2.95	_____	_____
Mark: Jesus' Works and Words—Large Print Study Guide (BWP001023)	$3.15	_____	_____
Mark:Jesus' Works and Words—Teaching Guide (BWP001024)	$3.45	_____	_____
Jesus in the Gospel of Mark—Study Guide (BWP000066)	$1.95	_____	_____
Jesus in the Gospel of Mark—Large Print Study Guide (BWP000065)	$1.95	_____	_____
Jesus in the Gospel of Mark—Teaching Guide (BWP000067)	$2.45	_____	_____
Luke: Journeying to the Cross—Study Guide (BWP000057)	$2.35	_____	_____
Luke: Journeying to the Cross—Large Print Study Guide (BWP000056)	$2.35	_____	_____
Luke: Journeying to the Cross—Teaching Guide (BWP000058)	$2.95	_____	_____
The Gospel of John: The Word Became Flesh—Study Guide (BWP001008)	$2.75	_____	_____
The Gospel of John: The Word Became Flesh—Large Print Study Guide (BWP001009)	$2.85	_____	_____
The Gospel of John: The Word Became Flesh—Teaching Guide (BWP001010)	$3.25	_____	_____
Acts: Toward Being a Missional Church—Study Guide (BWP001013)	$2.75	_____	_____
Acts: Toward Being a Missional Church—Large Print Study Guide (BWP001014)	$2.85	_____	_____
Acts: Toward Being a Missional Church—Teaching Guide (BWP001015)	$3.25	_____	_____
Romans: What God Is Up To—Study Guide (BWP001019)	$2.95	_____	_____
Romans: What God Is Up To—Large Print Study Guide (BWP001020)	$3.15	_____	_____
Romans: What God Is Up To—Teaching Guide (BWP001021)	$3.45	_____	_____

Ephesians, Philippians, Colossians—Study Guide (BWP001060)	$3.25	_____	_____
Ephesians, Philippians, Colossians—Large Print Study Guide (BWP001061)	$3.55	_____	_____
Ephesians, Philippians, Colossians—Teaching Guide (BWP001062)	$3.75	_____	_____
1, 2 Timothy, Titus, Philemon—Study Guide (BWP000092)	$2.75	_____	_____
1, 2 Timothy, Titus, Philemon—Large Print Study Guide (BWP000091)	$2.85	_____	_____
1, 2 Timothy, Titus, Philemon—Teaching Guide (BWP000093)	$3.25	_____	_____
Revelation—Study Guide (BWP000084)	$2.35	_____	_____
Revelation—Large Print Study Guide (BWP000083)	$2.35	_____	_____
Revelation—Teaching Guide (BWP000085)	$2.95	_____	_____

Coming for use beginning December 2008

Ezra, Haggai, Zechariah, Nehemiah, Malachi—Study Guide (BWP001071)	$3.25	_____	_____
Ezra, Haggai, Zechariah, Nehemiah, Malachi—Large Print Study Guide (BWP001072)	$3.55	_____	_____
Ezra, Haggai, Zechariah, Nehemiah, Malachi—Teaching Guide (BWP001073)	$3.75	_____	_____

Standard (UPS/Mail) Shipping Charges*	
Order Value	Shipping charge**
$.01—$9.99	$6.50
$10.00—$19.99	$8.00
$20.00—$39.99	$9.00
$40.00—$59.99	$10.00
$60.00—$79.99	$11.00
$80.00—$99.99	$12.00
$100.00—$129.99	$14.00
$130.00—$159.99	$18.00
$160.00—$199.99	$22.00
$200.00—$249.99	$26.00
$250.00—$299.99	$28.00
$300.00—$349.99	$32.00
$350.00—$399.99	$40.00
$400.00—$499.99	$48.00
$500.00—$599.99	$58.00
$600.00—$799.99	$70.00**

Cost of items (Order value) _____

Shipping charges (see chart*) _____

TOTAL _____

*Plus, applicable taxes for individuals and other taxable entities (not churches) within Texas will be added. Please call 1-866-249-1799 if the exact amount is needed prior to ordering.

**For order values $800.00 and above, please call 1-866-249-1799 or check www.baptistwaypress.org

Please allow three weeks for standard delivery. For express shipping service: Call 1-866-249-1799 for information on additional charges.

YOUR NAME

PHONE

YOUR CHURCH

DATE ORDERED

MAILING ADDRESS

CITY

STATE   ZIP CODE

MAIL this form with your check for the total amount to
BAPTISTWAY PRESS, Baptist General Convention of Texas,
333 North Washington, Dallas, TX 75246-1798
(Make checks to "Baptist Executive Board.")

OR, **FAX** your order anytime to: 214-828-5376, and we will bill you.

OR, **CALL** your order toll-free: 1-866-249-1799
(M-Th 8:30 a.m.-6:00 p.m.; Fri 8:30 a.m.-5:00 p.m. central time),
and we will bill you.

OR, **E-MAIL** your order to our internet e-mail address:
baptistway@bgct.org, and we will bill you.

OR, **ORDER ONLINE** at www.baptistwaypress.org.

We look forward to receiving your order! Thank you!